The Stripper, The Drug Dealer & The Bishop

Three Husbands, Same Spirit

Lydia Davis

The Stripper, The Drug Dealer & The Bishop

Copyright © 2016 by Lydia Davis

Library of Congress Control Number: 2017919017
ISBN: Paperback 978-0-692-98889-3

All rights reserved. No part of this book may be reproduced or transmitted in any form or by any means, electronic or mechanical, including photocopying, recording, or by any information storage or retrieval system, without permission in writing from the copyright owner.

The names and identifying characteristics of some of the individuals featured throughout this book have been changed to protect their privacy.

Printed in the United States of America.

To my mom, Tallie Davis who prayed for me and was with me every step of the way.

To my late father Eddie Lee Davis

To my daughters, Shelice (Chris) Davis Crowley and Sharron (Excell) Davis Haskins who hung in there with me in spite of myself; who never once denied me as their mother.

To my grandchildren, Javonta (great grandson Javon), Jaquiwn, Philip Beals Jr., Demetrius Beal (great grandson Niamiah), Arianna Beal, Jayla Crowley, Joryn Crowley.

To my late grandson, Savon Beal.

To my brothers, Donald (Evette) Davis and Jerome (Lena) Davis.

To my late brothers, Lamont Davis and Anton Davis.

To my late sisters, Valentina (Tina) and Cynthia Davis.

To my nieces and nephews, Lamont Jr., Cirrae, Deandre, Loris, Kyran, Jana, Jalisa, Jeremiah, Gregory, Thomas Jr.

To my younger cuz' who was always there with me Janet Daniel

To one of my best friends Denise Horne

Anne Davis Horton—who never stopped encouraging me to finish this book. Every day she would call me and ask, "Are you working on the book? Are you working on the book? Are you working on the book?"

To all my relatives and friends who walked this walk with me.

Thanks to Nat Crawford who started on this book as a ghost writer.

A very special thanks to my love, my friend, and my partner Edward J. Schilling, who not only helped me through my transition, but also helped me write this book.

And to the number one in my life, the author and finisher of my faith, my Lord, my Savior, Jesus Christ.

Contents

Childhood 1
Party Time 7
Move to Utah 13
The Cross 25
Jackie 29
Enter the Stripper 31
The Cats 37
The Stripper's Father 43
Bruce 47
Enter the Drug Dealer 51
The Killer Nurse 57
The Raid 61
A Man Came Up Behind Me 65
Happy Marriage Fading 67
Spike 69
Nan 71
Jackie and the Burglar 73
Worker Killed 75
Jackie's Sad End 79
Going to Church 81
Perfect Peace 83
Two of the Drug Dealer's Friends Attack 85
Drug Treatment 89
One Center was Real Nice 91
Five-Dollar Man 93
40 oz 95
How My Parents Raised My Kids 97
The Stench of Sin 99
My Gruesome Time in the Alleys 101
I Knew I Was Dying 103
My Father's Dream 105
Turning Point 107

Lamont	109
Lamont's Stroke	111
Move to Wisconsin	113
Second Husband's Girlfriend	117
She (My Sister) Always Said Good Things About Me	119
Living in Milwaukee—A Rehab Experience Like None Other	121
HIV Test	123
The Baby	125
The Taste of Cigarettes	127
Visiting Lamont	129
Anton's (Mickey's) Stroke	131
Mickey's Funeral	135
Insurance Agent	143
Lamont's Death	147
My Confidant, My Friend, My Sister Tina is Dead	151
Bible Studies	155
Sunday School Teacher and Choir	157
Enter the Bishop	159
Cynthia Dies	163
New House	165
Christmas Surprise	167
The Wedding Day	169
The Bishop's Wife	171
Evangelist Incident	173
Christian Academy	177
The Ordination	181
Fed Up with Wifely Duties	185
Benji	187
The Voice of God	189
Losing Everything	191
Put Out	193
Locked Out	195
Shut Out	199
A New Chapter	201
Final Words From The Author	209

Childhood

I was born and raised on the Westside of Chicago, and that environment would affect the rest of my life, exposing me to experiences and dangers that most are not able to survive. And most did not. My family, friends, foes, and heroes dropped like swatted flies all around me month after month, year after year, once I grew up and hit the streets running after fun. With each birthday I'd learn things I didn't expect to learn, I'd taste the things I'd observed from a distance, and surely I'd danced with the devil while I was at it because for sure I hadn't recognized him in his glamorous disguise—a disguise that hypnotized me.

See, my life was like most living the American dream. That is, on the inside of the walls of my home, it was my safe haven where love, music, and plenty of good food abounded. My mother and father were working parents and as far I could see through innocent eyes, we wanted for nothing. My mother worked nights and Daddy worked days and nights (he was never without two jobs). They weren't around much, but like magic we were all at the table every evening, and when I lifted my eyes toward the head of that long table, there sat my dad like a king on a throne. We passed the fried chicken and collard greens amongst us; the cornbread, macaroni and cheese, gravy, and sweet potatoes traveled the table and we ate to our fill. We washed our dinner down with Kool-Aid, then bum-rushed the dessert after every plate was clean. Daddy sat back in his chair, quiet and full like a satisfied overseer eyeing the goings-on of his family. I never gave it a second thought then, but looking back I'd have to say he was a heck of a man, especially since he worked so much yet frolicked with other tasty ladies endlessly. I don't know how he made it to the table for every single family dinner. Mom was fully aware that Daddy sat at our table with thoughts of other women on his mind and plans to disappear shortly after dinner the majority of the time. Regardless, she cooked delicious meals, worked a job, and kept a spotless home for us.

    I was the fifth of seven children, and how I adored my family, especially my older siblings. I seemed to have eyes for them only, so I'd barely noticed Daddy's absence. After all, he held down several jobs: he was either driving a cab or limo, as well as being a worker for the American Can Company. He couldn't have possibly been behaving disloyally all the time, I figured. With seven kids to feed and clothe, he snatched up work wherever he could and of course, as I said, Mom pulled her weight like a champ. Where was the loophole? How'd these side ladies get in? Where did he find the time?

    My oldest brothers were in the military, Vietnam in the '60s when I was between the ages of 9 and 11. Their visits home were the highlight of my days. They'd embarked on a world I'd never know, but when they came home they brought that world with them, and what a show it was for me. I would hide under the kitchen table and listen to their stories about getting drunk and having good times, partying. They didn't talk about military duties or heroic missions they'd been on at all. It was all about the partying. Not only did they tell the story, they lived it right before my eyes. Drinks flowed plenteously and I'd watch as they threw their heads back, bottles pressed to their parted, pursed lips, and suck down the intoxicating potion, all the while swaying to the music that played continuously. The music seemed to take them away as they sang and even harmonized together even though they'd become very drunk. Right away I made my identification with all of it. In fact, I projected myself to be years older than I was; my personal maturity couldn't arrive fast enough. I wanted to drink and be happy and sing with the best of them.

    From time to time my brothers Donald, Lamont, and Jerome, and friends Raymond, Maurice, Felton, and sometimes Walter, hung around the house listening to the likes of The Temptations, Gladys Knight & the Pips, Tyrone Davis, and

B.B. King, singing and playing a card game called bid whist. I was taking notes; I loved to watch and listen. It was going to be my turn in just a couple of years, or hopefully sooner. They partied with each other for hours, then got up and skipped off to the club. Or, when the time came, my brothers would go back to their military duties and I wouldn't see them anymore for many months. Nevertheless, no sooner than they'd left and I was finally alone, I stepped into their spot; it was my chance to put on those LPs and sing with the lyrics, wishing I were in the clubs, dancing to the music and drinking just like I knew they were. The one thing I could not deny was the love between my brothers. Drunk or sober, they loved each other sincerely. It had quite a positive effect on me. Looking back, it was easy for me to look up to my brothers with admiration because they were touchable and Daddy was not. Did Daddy love me and my brothers and sisters? Of course. But his absence was something we considered normal, especially since our mother never shed a tear over it nor uttered a foul or complaining word about it—not in front of us, anyway.

Me and my sister, Tina, who I loved dearly and was three years older than me, used to enjoy singing along to classic R & B tunes. Nothing could have tickled mine and my sister's funny bones like the new release of a song by the Temptations entitled "Papa Was a Rolling Stone." When we heard that song, we laughed and hollered, "That's Daddy! That's Daddy!" We learned every word and sang it often through our cracked-wide smiling faces.

One day, when I was about fourteen years old, I decided that at last I was in love, but for some reason I was too afraid to do as I'd been trained while watching from my observation spot under the table when I was nine, ten, eleven or so. Basically, I'd always been a creative child, fantasizing about writing books or pretending to sing like Gladys Knight or Aretha Franklin. So, what would my creative mind come up with to show that I was a grownup who could handle herself in a real life desire? Even though Daddy was not around much and was not affectionate at all, he managed to be around just enough to tell me not to mess with boys. "Don't mess with them boys, girl," he'd said several times without explanation in a very soft voice, but you always knew he meant what he said and said what he meant. But at least he could say he covered the sex talk all fathers have with their little girls. My mother has never mentioned a bird or a bee to this day, but she had a hawk eye and kept a ban on boys coming through our doors before a certain age. The reason my sister could entertain a boy at home was because she had reached *that* age. In her reaching that golden age, I was provided with one-on-one lessons in having a good time. I was allowed to hang with them and have fun singing, playing cards, and laughing as if I were one of the girls.

I quietly continued to observe and take in the behavior of my older siblings. The older I got, the looser they seemed to behave around me. At times, my sister and her boyfriend would pop candy looking things that I knew were not headache pills. They would chuck down these pills as if they were indescribably delicious. I asked what they were and if I could have some too. "Girl, you don't know nothin' about this," I'd hear.

"Well, I'd like to know. They don't really look like aspirin. What is it?" I asked.

"Strawberry dabs," they answered.

"What's it for?" I asked.

"Oh, it's just something to keep you alert, that's all."

Then before I knew it, they'd pulled out something else and choked that down too. I looked and I listened but I wanted to taste and eventually I did.

I had a little sister eleven years younger than me that I felt very responsible for. After all, I'd washed her diapers on a scrub board the whole time she was in them and learned to cook and clean to ensure that she was covered during my parents' long absences. My older siblings were teaching me a lot and I wanted to be sure she wasn't taught as well. I loved my sister dearly, and here I was, left to be her mirror. Uh-oh.

At the tender age of fourteen, education was supposed to be the crux of my existence and the thing that would shape me for doing well in life. This certainly was not something I could live out all smiles before my young sibling because I hated school so much. Mom sometimes had to beat me with a broom to get me out of bed to go. If she hadn't, I would have laid there all day and not gotten up at all, at least not for school. In all, my grades weren't bad but, oh, how I hated going!

I loved fifth grade. My teacher's name was Mrs. Hanna. She used to play the piano, and one of my dreams was to play the piano. I remember I used to ask my mom "Can I take piano lessons?" and she'd apologize because we just couldn't afford it. By the time I was in sixth grade I had Mrs. Rice. She was the meanest white teacher I ever had. Mrs. Rice made me through with school. By the time I got to seventh and eighth grade I was at the top of my class, but I wouldn't go to school. I had to take summer school to graduate out of eighth grade. That was the end of my high school education. I may have been in the building but was never in a classroom. I felt that there was too much else to do with my life, like party, dance, sing, pop my pills, and date boys. And if anyone asked how I'd come up with such a notion, I could easily point to my examples. They appeared to be doing just fine with this alternative.

Party Time

The time came at last when I could see what a good party really was. I had turned fifteen and was finally free to taste and see! At this time I was still taking strawberry dabs, but beer, Boone's Farm wine, and cigarettes became my vices and I enjoyed them. Nothing gave me joy like dancing and hanging out at the bar. In fact by sixteen I had become a barmaid and, believe it or not, still a virgin. Partying was too good to be true and I stayed in party mode for years, stopping only twice to give birth to my daughters and to get married to my first husband.

By seventeen I had laid my virginity out at the feet of my boyfriend as a keepsake offering for our relationship. He was not the first boyfriend I'd had by now; I'd dated a guy much older who I'd denied the pleasure of my petite body, and as a result he'd left me for a girl who freely gave up hers, booty and all. So, when this new boyfriend (who I will call Jim) and I became a couple, naturally I felt obligated to please in order to keep him. Reluctantly, I gave in. I'll never forget the first time when he penetrated me; nothing could have been more painful. I hated it. I didn't know why everybody was so excited about having sex. To me, my first experience was nothing but pure pain. But I had a boyfriend.

Living out what I'd admired in my older siblings had its ups and downs, and they'd left out the part about what it would cost me. My boyfriend, however, had other ideas. He had me dressed in my buttcrack-high shorts, halters, and heels, and had me prance about and was duly noticed. He had great ambition and wanted me to be a part of his life's blueprint. He had delusions of being a pimp and I'd be his first prostitute! I fought tooth and nail against his ghastly plans. The first time he dropped me off on a street corner to turn tricks, as soon as he drove off I ran into a nearby bar to hide out. I *hated* being put out on the street. I *hated* being set out as a prostitute. I was afraid. I nervously tried getting attention from passing cars. I don't know who was going to pick me up—what kind of person or abuse I might have to endure from them. They may want to kill me and I would be able to do nothing about it and nobody would find me. And besides, I hated sex at the time because I was so petite and it still was painful for me.

The second time he put me out there, I didn't realize he was watching me. When I came out of the bar I was hiding in, he was waiting for me. I told him I didn't make any money because nobody wanted me. "Get yo black ass in this car, bitch!" he yelled. I saw yo mutha fuckin' ass runnin' to that bar! Bitch, you ain't tryin' to make my money! You tryin' to make a damn fool out of me?" He took me back to his apartment and told me, "You get yo' ass in that bedroom! I got something for you bitch! Get yo' ass up against that wall bitch." (I've never been this many bitches in my life! Where I was raised, we didn't talk like this.) Just the way he spoke to me terrorized me. He positioned himself on the other side of the room, reached into his waist, and pulled out a .32 revolver and fired it at me! That bullet missed my head by only a couple of inches! All I saw was fire and smoke and I fell to the floor. I thought I was dead! The shot was so close and so loud it even scared him! It could only have been God's protection causing that bullet to miss me. Do you see him?

When he composed himself and helped me up he said, "You get back out there and go get my money bitch!"

I thought, Where did all of this come from? I was just all about partying and having fun!

For a couple of days I hid in my family's house and didn't come out. When I finally came out, I felt I was safe and made my way to the bar, but there he was, waiting for me sitting on the corner and saying, "Where you been, bitch? Get yo ass back out there on that corner and make me my money!"

That night, while I was on "duty," my dear father came whizzing by in his 1970 Cadillac Seville. I believe we both pretended not to see each other. That night, when I got home, daddy and I went down a telepathic road together, avoided eye contact, and agreed to say nothing. He had known what was going on and I knew it. Strangely, this was a comfort to me. So much for the strength of his *sex talk* with me years before.

Later that evening, while I was on the street, this white man pulled up and he said, "Do you wanna party?" I got in because I knew I was being watched. I remember being told the next time the bullet wouldn't miss. Once inside the car, I quickly told my story. "Please help me. I'm not a prostitute. Someone is making me do this. Please give me some money so I have something to give him." He felt so sorry for me that he didn't do anything with me and gave me 20 dollars. I thanked him and quickly got out the car and gave it to the pimp. His eyes lit up like he thought, *Wow! I'm really on my way as a big-time pimp!* He took my 20 dollars and he said, "I'll see you the same time tomorrow." That 20 dollars must have been burning a hole in his pocket! *What a cheap, dumb pimp!* I thought. *He's not putting me out on the street again.*

The next night I went to the bar instead of the street—I don't know how I got past him—and when I wanted to go home, the DJ offered me a ride in his car. Just as my girlfriend Debra and I were getting into the DJ's car, the would-be pimp (ain't) drove up with his crew and yelled, "You get in this car, bitch!" When I saw him, I felt heavy fear sinking in my stomach and thought, *Oh God!* The DJ got scared, made us all get out of the car, locked it, and went back into the bar, leaving my girlfriend and I standing there outside the car. My girlfriend was also scared, so she hastily said "Call out to me if you need me." and also went back into the bar.

Now I was alone on the street, facing the pimp and his crew. He then grabbed me and threw me into his car saying, "Get in that car bitch!" All I could see was a flash of that bullet flying past my head from before. I was sure I was going to die that night, That pimp was crazy!

They took me to the nearest park. We got out, he took all the money I had from my pockets, and he beat me and left me there. I made it home, bloodied and beaten, and when my parents saw how beat up I was, they put me on the first plane to Montana, where my sister now lived, and went looking for this guy with guns at the ready. I stayed out there for a few months.

When I got home and I ran into the pimp (ain't), he said something like, "No hard feelings. You wasn't workin' out anyway." I think he was trying to save face since he knew my family was looking for him.

It was a few years later when I ran into him again and he told me how he missed me, how he loved me, and how he had four women in his stable and was adding more women. He invited me to come with him to "check out his crib" and said he knew how I hated being on the street, so I could be his "main lady" and service only him so I wouldn't have to work the street. I thought to myself, *What a dumb pimp!*

My life became one big party after I escaped the would-be pimp. I hung out at the bar a lot and became friends with the bartender, who I'll call Chuck. He always loaded me up with my favorite drinks and soon became my confidante. Ultimately he and I became an *item*. I was 19 at that time and still living at home then. From there my partying friends began to fall off, leaving me skimming for new party blood.

While Chuck the bartender dated everyone who came into the bar, and while pregnant with Chuck's child, I became friends with Rob, whom I met in the bar where Chuck worked. After having my first baby girl, Rob became a father figure to her. Chuck never even offered to buy diapers for her, and at the time I didn't have the sense to make him buy them.

I remember the events around my first child's birth. When my water broke, my father took me to the hospital. After thirty-six hours of labor, the doctors realized I needed a caesarean section because my pelvis bone was too small for her tiny little head to fit through. When my child was delivered, she weighed four pounds and eleven ounces, and they said she had jaundice and some other things wrong, so they needed to keep her in the hospital. In those days, you stayed at the hospital a week after caesarean sections. When I went home, my baby was still very sick and they had to keep her. When I got home from the hospital I began to have headaches. I had complained about headaches for three days, and on the third day after getting out of bed, I walked down the hall into our dining/family room and I suddenly had a really bad pain in my head. It stopped me in my tracks and I put my hands on my head. My younger brother Anton, the soon-to-be preacher, said, "What is wrong with you?"

I said, "I don't know—I just have *such* a bad headache. My head is throbbing—it feels like it's going to explode." After that, I passed out, fell to the floor and began going into convulsions. I remember hearing my dad say, "Quick! Get me a spoon to put in her mouth so she don't bite her tongue!" My daddy was never home, but look at God—my daddy was home that day. I remember hearing later how the ambulance took so long to get there that he drove me to the hospital himself and ran several red lights to get me there. He was known to be a fast driver, but my mom said she was never so scared in her life, the way he went through those red lights.

I was in and out of consciousness and remember my mother looking over me in the hospital bed. I began to have another seizure and I heard her scream, "Somebody help! She's having another seizure!"

Weeks went by. When my consciousness came back enough to know what was going on and where I was, I looked around and saw all of these other people sharing the same room with me who had brain surgery and thought they all looked like their mind was taken somehow.

The doctors called my family into the room to discuss my condition and told me they had good news. They told me the tests came back showing my spinal fluid had blood in it, which told them I had a brain aneurysm that had either burst or was hemorrhaging. They said although the condition was serious, the good news was they could save me with an operation. They explained what they were going to do and that they needed to operate as soon as possible.

After seeing those other people, plus finding out the hospital had "research hospital" in its name, it made me think, *They're experimenting on those people! If they operate on me I'll never be the same! Well, they're not experimenting on me!*

My father said, "What you want to do, girl? It's up to you."

I said, "I want to get out of this hospital, take my baby, and go home!" During all this time since having my baby girl a month ago, she was still hospitalized. The doctors said if I wanted to leave I would have to sign myself out, and if I did that they would not be responsible for anything that happened to me. So not only did I sign myself out, I signed my baby out too. Within an hour I got my baby and we went home. As I signed out and was leaving, the doctors said, "If you sign yourself out, we can't save you! You'll be lucky if you reach thirty! If you don't have this operation, you'll need to get an angiograph every year to check the spinal fluid to make sure the aneurysm isn't hemorrhaging. Just because you don't see it, doesn't mean it's not there."

Now I know the meaning of *All sickness is not unto death.* Even though at the time I didn't realize it, it was God. There he is again. Do you see him?

Move to Utah

The way the events of my life were unfolding, it was looking very much like partying would become the last thing I would enjoy for quite a while. In fact, the next thing I knew I was twenty years old, in a new relationship, and moving to Logan, Utah! My new boyfriend Rob, my little girl, and I moved in with Rob's brother and sister-in-law and their daughter Jen, who was about four or five years old at the time. This girl was cute as a button but I soon realized she was (there's no other way to put it) a demon seed. The devil! She was extremely devious and was always doing things to my daughter. The last straw was when Jen stacked milk crates on top of each other on our third-floor apartment balcony. I just happened to walk out onto the balcony when Jen proceeded to help my daughter up onto the crates and then start to push her over the edge! If I hadn't stopped her, she would have pushed my daughter to her death! Yes—she was trying to kill my daughter! All I could think of was my poor daughter's brains scattered on the pavement below. I remember the look in Jen's eyes when I stopped her: she looked at me as if to say, "What? I wasn't gonna do nothin'." After that incident, that was it, we had to move.

At that time, my boyfriend became a student at Logan State University in Utah. Since he was a student, my boyfriend and I were able to get an off-campus apartment of our own. That's where my new life began—bored to tears. Since we lived in a house across from a cemetery, I spent much of my time at the window watching internments day after day. That was as exciting as it got. There was no more Chicago in my view.

As our domestic relationship developed, my boyfriend began acting like a controlling and oppressive husband. He bossed me around and wouldn't allow for everyday norms like eating and dropping a crumb or two; I could barely finish swallowing what I'd eaten before he demanded that I wash my dish and utensils. I felt like a cross between Dorothy in the strangest Kansas ever and Cinderella being bossed about by a wicked step-husband! When we were in Chicago he was a drinkin', marijuana smokin', heroin usin' partier. Now all of our partying, drinking, and drugging had stopped cold. He himself did not take a single drink or smoke a single reefer either. The only liberty we took was smoking cigarettes; I smoked Kools while he enjoyed Viceroys.

Another part of his oppressive nature I didn't like, which spilled over to our sexual relationship, was how he always wanted it and wanted it fast and hard. What I meant was, sex wasn't pleasing with him because it was painful—I was very small and he was very well endowed, and he didn't care that it hurt me. I'm going to take an aside here. Men: Those of you who are well endowed, please be sensitive to the woman's pleasure and comfort. Please ask them, "Am I hurting you? Should I go slow? Should I not push so hard?" Size is not all you need for a successful sexual relationship. All men regardless of size: It's not the size but consideration and sensitivity to the woman's pleasure and comfort that matters. God made us so that we can make it work with whatever each of us has, regardless of size, if we care about the other person and if we're willing to work at it. And women: Don't be afraid to tell a man he is hurting you. You shouldn't have to pretend pleasure for fear of damaging the relationship. We need to establish healthy, balanced relationships with each other.

In no time I was pregnant and begging to return to Chicago because of the fact that I was prone to seizures and had to have cesareans—or at least that was the convenient excuse I leaned on. Since I had a cesarean when I gave birth the first time, I figured why not turn it into a vehicle to ride out of Utah on? Because this town was too quiet, too dead, and too sleepy. I still had some party left in me.

I had nothing else, so I relentlessly pushed and pressed against my boyfriend's better wishes. "I just can't have my baby here! I gotta go back home to Chicago! The doctors here in Utah don't know my medical history—about the caesareans, the aneurysms, the seizures." I wasn't just using that as an excuse to go back to Chicago—I was afraid. I kept remembering the doctors back in Chicago when they diagnosed me as having brain aneurysms. I kept hearing them in my mind saying "You won't make it past thirty." The fear was real. I was scared. I needed to go home to Chicago to have this baby.

It took me about eight months of pregnancy to convince him I needed to go home. Reluctantly, he helped me pack my things to go home, and I promised to return after I had my baby.

I arrived back home to my beloved Westside, safe within the warm walls of my mom and dad's apartment. After giving birth I remained at home for another month, then secured my own apartment which was walking distance from my parents. That's when both my boyfriend and I knew I wasn't coming back to Utah. I remember talking to him on the phone, and he was saying, "If you were coming back, why did you get an apartment?"

I said, "I need to be at home for some more time to make sure both me and my baby will be okay. I want to make sure I don't have another seizure and make sure my baby won't have any more medical problems." He called me a number times trying to get me to come back and I always had an excuse. I would say "I don't have the money to come down there" and he didn't have enough to send for me. Things were getting really hard for him in Utah. After finishing school and getting a job, it just wasn't working out for him, so he moved to Las Vegas. Finally I agreed to come down there and we got enough money together for plane fare, and so I figured I'd be staying with him at his apartment. Just before coming down, I was talking on the phone with him, saying how we were going to have so much fun, how we'll finally be able to spend some time together, and how he was going to finally see his new daughter. During this conversation, it came up that he was not living in his own apartment but was now living with some friends and wouldn't have room for me and my daughters. We would need to stay in a hotel. After agreeing what hotel I'd be staying at, we set our plans and all we needed to do was pay for it. And then came the revelation of his deception all this time which hit me like a ton of bricks: He said, "I'm sorry, but when you come down, I won't be able to spend any nights with you at the hotel." And when I asked why, he said, "I have another woman and she likes me to be at home at night." He was just that cold and blunt. No need to say it, but neither I or my daughters ever saw or spoke to him again.

My baby girls and I made our home on the third floor, accessed only by three long flights of stairs. Those were some invigorating, tiring days as I carried groceries and babies up and down those steps regularly. The good thing was my body was whipped back into shape quickly.-

It was easy for me to make friends, which I did readily; they came along with all the booze and marijuana I wanted. All the frolic was returning to my life in good fashion. But no one could question my parenting skills because there is where I drew the line; my partying would not interrupt their innocence—yet. They were always first on my heart and mind. For instance, when things got awkward, I'd pick up and move and continued to do so a couple of more times for the comfort of my small family. My last move would be the place I felt the coziest. Stability met me there.

I started to feel lonely, so I started smoking marijuana and I met this guy that lived down the street that sold it. His wife was a nurse. One day I came to their house to buy a bag and her son, who I will call "Dee," and who I'd never seen before, answered the door. He was the most attractive light-skinned man I ever saw. At his mother's suggestion, we began to spend time together. Days became months and we soon moved in together. I had never seen Dee without his books. I was told he was going to school to become a nurse as his mother was. Day after day, Dee would take his books and head off to school as I set off to work. After a while, I let his female cousin move in with us. One day, she confronted me about money for her aid check being missing. When I finally convinced her I didn't take it, and that I had money coming up missing also, she said, "Oh, I know what happened. Dee's been stealing from me just like he's stealing from you!"

I said, "Oh my God! I never guessed he was stealing from me! How did he even know where I hid my money?"

She told me, "He figured it out by counting your footsteps." When I opened my stash of money at night, he pretended to be asleep and listened for the number of footsteps I took when I got out of bed and listened for drawers opening or any noise that would reveal where my money was. After hearing that, whenever I would get my money I would walk all over the house, open random drawers and closets and do all sorts of things to throw him off. When I did that, my money stopped disappearing. Dee's cousin told me truth after shocking truth about him. She told me he was never in any school after high school. I said, "That's impossible, he knows so much about nursing. How would he know all that if he's not going to school?"

"He reads his mom's nursing books on his own and learned that stuff." She told me. Then, the final, biggest shock of all. She said, "You know he was in jail right?" and I said, "Yeah, for drugs."

"No, not for drugs! For murder!" she said. I thought he was messing with me when he once told me he killed a cab driver just to see what it felt like to kill someone, and I just laughed and said, "Naw! You never killed anyone!" But he would insist on explaining how the cab driver begged for his life, and he just shot him cold bloodedly in the back of the head, and the taxi driver died.

After I heard this, I confronted him on this and several other things his cousin told me. He freely admitted to murder, telling me, "Well, I already told you I killed someone." After the confrontation, he put his cousin out, and a few weeks later, I put him out. Why did it take so long to put him out? Each time I brought up him leaving, he said he'd get me. And I believed him—I knew he already killed someone before. I threatened to put my brothers on him, and he finally agreed to leave.

Looking back, I am amazed at how God must have been protecting me from this sociopath, an extremely intelligent, devious, and abusive monster with no conscience or remorse. He could have coldly decided to kill me or my children at any time and may have been able to get away with it.

My mother worked at Brach's candy for many years, along with my sister, before she moved to Montana. Therefore, I got a job there too and was feeling like settling down. I'd met a new boyfriend at work and was feeling pretty hopeful. I worked in the office and he worked in the factory. I'd be working at my desk and I'd always see him standing by the elevator, smiling at me. I was hesitant to date him at first because I knew he had been dating this other girl at the company. But as it turns out, he was no friend at all, he just needed a booty call. Our sexually convenient relationship went on for a few months, which of course caused him to put reigns on me that I wasn't going to stand for much longer, especially knowing that he was not going to be a serious life partner. Soon I grew tired of his using me and just wanted to be alone until the right man came along.

Time passed and he was fading into the "just friends" category of my life. However, unknown to me, he was stalking me, watching my every move, even peeping into my apartment window where he'd seen me with friends. One day he invited me to a card party to play Bid Whist, a game he knew I loved. Of course I said "Yes, I'll be there. When I arrived at the so-called card party, no one seemed to be in attendance but me, him, and one other guy friend of his. My girlfriend Carmen was also invited but had not arrived yet, and strangely, no other ladies, nor guys for that matter, showed up either.

"Where's everybody?" I asked.

"Oh, they're coming. Let's start a game and play 'til they get here," he said. Out came the cards, and as soon as I saw that they were not Bee brand cards, I felt strange. In fact when I looked closer, I saw that the cards had photos of naked women printed on them. Immediately, I knew I was in trouble; I wanted to run. As calmly as I could I said to them, "I think

I'll go home now. Since there are not enough players I'll just come back when some more people come." I was ignored as my ex-boyfriend got up and locked the big brown door. The sound of the lock securing the door nearly took my breath away. The look in his eyes, his mannerisms and behavior totally changed from the way I knew him. This little mild-mannered factory worker who pleasantly smiled at me when we first met had changed from Dr Jekyll to Mr. Hyde, a dangerous, aggressive monster. I knew there wasn't a chance of me getting out. I begged to go home to no avail. After a very short while he disappeared into the bathroom, leaving me alone with his friend who didn't seem to be as crazy as he was. "Help me! Please, help me!" I begged the friend. All he could say to me was, "But I can't. I can't do nothin'. He'll get me too." Then my heart dropped.

When my ex returned from the bathroom, he gave his friend the eye and the two of them snatched me from the dining room table and dragged me to the bedroom, then slammed me down on a sheetless bed and one at a time pounced on me like animals going in for the kill. They violated and defiled me horribly. Beneath their smelly pumping bodies I wondered how I would ever get out.

After a while they took a break to sit there, smoking cigarettes and gawking at me laying there like acquired bounty and crying, pleading, "Please let me go. Let me go home." They held a conversation as if I wasn't even present. "Let's get her in the ass now," my ex said. Terror filled me. I nearly fainted. I knew that would be my breaking point; there was no way I'd survive that kind of contamination, so my mind went back to when I was in the hospital and convulsing while having a seizure, and that's when I decided it was seizer time. I had seizures before, so I knew how to act like I was having one, and I always wanted to be an actress, so this was the best role I ever played (it had to be or I would die).

During their cigarette break, my ex left the room to go into the bathroom. I felt now was my chance. I began shaking and crying. The friend looked scared and said, "What's wrong with you?"

I said, "I feel like I'm going into convulsions—I was diagnosed years ago with a brain aneurysm which causes seizures, and if it leaks I could die any moment!" By the time my ex came back into the room I was into my full seizure act: severe shaking, my eyes rolled back, my mouth open.

My ex looked at me and said, "What the hell is happening?"

The friend was now terrified. "She's going into convulsions and she could have a brain aneurism and die! Man, we gotta get her out of here! If she dies we'll go to jail for murder as well as rape! Let's get her out of here!"

It scared them to death but it saved my life. They quickly dressed me, put me in a car, and took me home, dropping me out front. "Get the fuck out of this car bitch!" my ex said, with a dead look in his eye. "If you ever tell anyone about this, I'll not only kill you but your daughters too! Now get the fuck out my car."

It was a couple weeks later before I saw him again. It seemed he was avoiding me because I usually saw him every day at work. One day, I was at work and went to the cafeteria where my mom worked on the third shift. I was on my way out of the cafeteria after just having lunch when I ran into him coming in along with a group of other guys. He put on the biggest, phoniest smile on his face and he said, "Hey! How ya doing?" I couldn't look him in eye or speak. The other guys said, "What's wrong with her?" and my ex said, "I don't know what's wrong with that crazy broad." (What happened to *bitch*?)

I walked past them down the hall back to my department, and all I could think about was what had happened in that house—the rape. That's all I could see. With overwhelming anger and tears in my eyes, I turned around and went back to the cafeteria. When I got there, he was just sitting down with his tray. I starting screaming at the top of my lungs, "You raped me! You raped me! You and your friend! Y'all raped me!" Stunned by my screaming, everyone in the cafeteria turned to see who I was talking about.

He yelled back, "What are you talking about? I didn't do anything!" A commotion was stirring in the cafeteria of Brach's candy company as embarrassment and anger burned straight through me. What made matters worse was that my mother's coworkers who also worked at the cafeteria had to witness all of this. Everyone knew my mother and saw her on a daily basis, which added to the embarrassment for both my mother and me.

As I continued to scream "You raped me!" he got up from the table he was sitting at, put his tray on the conveyor belt, and began to walk down the hall, all the while with me following him and screaming "You raped me." I followed him, repeatedly screaming "You raped me!" until he got on the elevator to his floor. They told me I could go home for the rest of the day. I don't remember how long before I returned to work. The humiliation and embarrassment I felt for my mother's pain was unbearable. It was worse than the rape that happened to me.

From that day on things were no longer the same; coworkers were talking and looking at me cockeyed. Word had apparently gotten back to the head of the company and my ex-boyfriend-turned-rapist, was terminated on the spot.

After he was fired, he stalked me. I would see him outside my apartment, watching me, or I'd see him drive by many days. One day I was looking out my apartment window and he drove up and said, "I'm gonna get you bitch! I'm gonna kill your motherfucking ass! What I did to you then was nothin' compared to what I'm gonna do to you!" I felt terror at the pit of my stomach. I knew he was serious. This man was crazy. I couldn't sleep at night. I was up all night, terrified at every sound. When I wanted to go anywhere I'd cautiously look out the window looking for anything that looked like his car or anyone that looked like him. I knew either I was going to die or something had to happen to stop him. No other possibilities were in sight. I was so scared I quit my job.

Another reason I quit was for peace's sake and to spare my mother undue shame. I felt awful because my mother was well respected there and had worked there for many years without incident and had in fact gotten me and my sister our jobs there. Now I had embarrassed her and myself. I had to leave, people were still talking; I'd become a sore within the company, a subject of company gossip. I so loved my mother and didn't want to be the cause of any more embarrassment, so I thought leaving was best.

The next clear thing I remember about that old boyfriend and his buddy was hearing that they had gotten killed by the police during a drug raid. They were shooting at the police and the police shot back and killed both of them. A girlfriend of mine had come running to me, asking if I'd heard that my old boyfriend was dead and was I going to the funeral. I snapped, "No! I would spit in his face if I go! It's best that I stay away." Admittedly, I was kind of glad that the chances of me seeing either one of them again had become impossible. This is the first time I can remember wanting anybody dead.

After my ex-boyfriend's death I also found out that he and his friend had done what he did to me to several other girls he dated at the candy factory, but they didn't say anything because they were terrified of him and knew he would kill them.

Just imagine, if I had stayed connected to that boyfriend—the monster that he truly was—my fate could have been much worse. God my Father looked over me in ways that my own father could not. He seemed to always have subtle ways of watching over me; His protection was unrecognizable and remained that way throughout my troubled life. Once again, death was knocking at my door, and once again I had a healer who had a hedge of protection around me.

It wasn't until after the fact that I realized what a monster he was. I thought about how *none* of the many other women he raped *ever* spoke a word against him. If he could put that much fear into so many people, it shows that everyone knew how dangerous he was. If he could threaten his friend into raping me even though he didn't want to, it showed how intimidating he could be. If he was willing to have a shoot-out with the police, it shows his disregard for his own life—how crazy he was. I could still see those eyes of death of his stabbing into me as he vowed to kill me. I shuddered as I thought about just how close to death I was. Thank you, Lord.

The Cross

My baby brother, Rev. Anton Davis, was nine years old when he gave his life to the Lord. He used to put messages under my pillow about the God he had found. He didn't want to leave me behind. In the '60s, instead of thinking about God like my brother wanted, I was more interested in watching *Creature Feature* on TV with Frankenstein, the Wolf Man, and the Mummy. My brother, on the other hand, didn't like that stuff at all. In fact he was scared of it. My favorite joke I'd play on him was to record the scary music from that show on a small tape recorder and when he would get up from bed to go to the bathroom at night, I would put that recorder under his bed and turn on the scary music. When he heard that, he would run out of the room, yelling, "Mom! Lil's back under my bed again with that *Creature Feature* music and scaring me!" She would come in with her faithful broom and make me get out from under the bed. I thought that was hysterical. I didn't understand my brother: his favorite things were to read the Bible and watch the Chicago Blackhawks hockey team. What black person watched hockey in the '60s?

Despite my fondness for Creature Feature and scaring my brother, I found myself sticking my head in the church door every now and then. My brother graduated from the Moody Bible Institute, received his master's degree and found his wife. He then became assistant pastor of King David Missionary Baptist Church on the west side of Chicago, where the pastor was Clarence Guyton.

I remember I went to one of the services my brother was preaching. I saw what looked like a projector shining the figure of a white cross onto the bottom of his robe. I looked around the church for what could be projecting this cross onto his robe and could find no source for it. I saw a small cross-shaped window in the church door behind me and thought maybe it was coming from there, but the one in the door was too small and at the wrong angle to project such a big cross at the bottom of his robe. I began figuring out the angles and positions of every window in the church that could possibly cause what I saw but could find nothing that would account for it. I thought it was so brilliant that there was no way everyone else didn't see that cross. I doubted the reality of what I saw. *This can't be real*, I thought. Then, as I felt my doubts about what I saw, the cross began disappearing piece by piece, maintaining its shape as a cross. Bit by bit, a piece would disappear—first from the top of the cross, then a piece that looked like it was the same size disappeared from the bottom of the cross, then from one side and then the other. Each piece that disappeared would always look like the same size. When enough pieces disappeared, only a square that made up the middle of the cross remained. It hung there for a minute and then it disappeared completely. I was looking around the church to see if anybody's mouth was hanging open in surprise or shock like mine was. Everyone else's expression had not changed—like they didn't see what I saw.

    After the service I got in the car with my brother, my mother, and my sister-in-law, Julie (my brother's wife), and didn't say a word because what I saw freaked me out. Once we were all in the car, Julie asked, "Did anyone see that cross?" and I yelled with joy, "Yes! I saw that cross! Did anyone else see it?" My mother and brother responded, "What cross?" Julie explained what she saw was the same as what I saw, but she didn't see it disappear. I said, "It must have come from that window" and she firmly said, "No way! It wasn't no window!" She told me how she mentally figured out the angles and positions of all the windows in the church and it couldn't have been from any window. When I told her how I saw it disappear, she definitely believed it was God—That God was showing himself through this brilliant cross of light, like he was saying, "Do you see me? Do you see me?" and when the last piece hung there, it was like God saying one last time, "Do you see me now?" and then God finally took it away.

What I saw in the church was the first of many experiences of God showing me something extraordinary and then, before satan could make me think I was just imagining things, God would always put someone else around who experienced the same thing as confirmation that it really did happen—that God is real. He would also show me something beyond what those that merely confirmed my experience experienced themselves in order to show me God was doing something uniquely for me. This wouldn't be the last time something like this would happen to me. Different things would happen again and again. Each time, God would put someone around me who would confirm what I experienced.

It was months later before I returned to another service at the church where the pastor Rev. Clarence Guyton spoke that day. I explained to him about the cross I saw and he told me what it meant. He said it meant it was time for me to pick up my cross and follow Jesus. I got scared and I thought to myself, *Pick up my cross? What cross? I ain't got no cross! Is Jesus out to get me? I don't see him—he's up in heaven. Does he want me to follow him to heaven? Am I gonna die?* I ran as though I was running for my life. It was a long time before they saw me again in that church! I reacted this way because I wasn't saved at the time and didn't understand what I was being told. I learned years later from studying Matthew 16:24 which said (from the King James version): "Then Jesus said unto his disciples, If any man will come after me, let him deny himself, and take up his cross, and follow me."

What picking up your cross and following him meant is to become a new person; to give up your old ways that are harmful to yourself and others and commit yourself to the good, Godly ways of love, compassion, humility, and servitude—To do what *God* wants you to do and not what *you* want to do. It means to acknowledge him in all your ways and let him direct your path. If you're reading this book and you don't know Jesus, he's talking to you now. It's time for *you* to pick up *your* cross and follow him. Stop right here and say, "Yes, Lord."

Jackie

I had a cat named Jackie. My girls and I loved her as much as any family member. My oldest daughter actually became Jackie's caretaker. She claimed Jackie as her own.

I remember when I first found her: One cold day I was rushing the kids to school (I was always late getting the kids to school) and on the way we saw this little bitty black-and-white kitten with a white face and a crooked black mustache on the curb. The kids got so excited. "Look at that kitten! It's so cute! Can we keep it?" I said, "I'm not taking that kitten. I don't know whose cat it is." My kids pleaded with me, so I said, "If that kitten is still here when I go home after dropping you off, I'll take it home." Sure enough, the kitten was still there, so I took it home.

Enter the Stripper

By the time I turned twenty-seven, my two little girls who I adored were in grade school. I remember once, I was on my way to pick up my daughter from school. As I approached the school at around 3:00 p.m., when classes were over for the day, I noticed there were no people around—nobody! I thought to myself, *Where is everybody?* No teachers, no students, nobody! When I got near the school entrance, out of the corner of my eye, I saw a little head pop out from around the building corner and disappear behind it again. When I investigated, I found it was my daughter, standing there all by herself. I asked her, "Why are you here all by yourself?"

"The teacher said school was going to end early today and they let everyone out." she replied.

"Did you see your teacher leave?"

"I saw her get in her car and drive away." She said.

"Why didn't you go home?"

"You told me not to walk home by myself." I realized they had let class out early and they never told me. I was so furious! I couldn't help but think of what could have happened to my little girl out there in this crazy world. Those thoughts made me shudder. To this day, every time I pass by that school, I think about that incident. This is one of many times I'm going to thank God for saving her!

I do miss the years when my bid whist partners Felton, his wife Evelyn, and I used to go out and dance and party together, but now I worked more and partied less, to the dismay of my partying friends. Believe it or not, I was housebound for the most part and grew to prefer it that way. One Friday evening, my best girlfriend Julie, who had had enough of my new life change, called me up and invited me out. Naturally I declined her invitation, citing motherly duties. She pressed in further and would not take no for an answer. She had rattled my nerves so that the next thing I knew I had gotten a babysitter and was on my way to party with her at some club of her choosing.

Although it was a nice change for me to get out and take in the scene again, to do something I'd never enjoyed before, the evening plans were all up to her and I followed along unenthused. Before I knew it, she'd lead me through the doors of a club where men took the stage, giving the audience a spectacular show with pounds of sweaty, gyrating, chocolate flesh. It didn't take me long to realize that I was in the pit of a male strip club. Men commanded the stage, pumping and dancing like nothing I'd ever seen before. In all my neighborhood wiles and travels, why hadn't I come across this? These guys danced in scanty costumes that really consisted of nothing more than a thong that depicted all types of characters, even military men, then stripped down to even less to reveal the bare guts of their girth. A pretty impressive penile show if I say so myself. They proudly flopped their gonads like flags in blustering wind! I sat in my seat with my eyes popped and my mouth wide open with water dripping down my cheeks. I was in drool heaven! I laughed nervously at the spectacles. Their taut bodies glistened with a film of perspiration that shone like crystal and twinkled in wide eyes. My eyes could scarcely keep up from one rolling set of hips to the next. The music was hypnotic, the sound of the screaming, howling women curled my ears, but my eyes took it all in and I was officially having a good time.

There was no confusion about why the women had packed this place out or why they smiled from the time they walked through the door until the time they went home. There was enough joy in that place to get any woman through her workweek and back again for the next weekend. My girlfriend loved this place and obviously frequented it to the point where she was familiar with some of the strippers. One stripper in particular seemed to have a charm about him that waved at me clear to my seat. His dancing was not like the others' either. He seemed almost gifted to move the way he did. His dancing was hypnotizing and a bit stimulating. I couldn't take my eyes off of him, and apparently he spotted me in the audience and made me his focus for the evening.

In between acts, my friend and I remained at our table drinking, laughing, and talking about what we'd just seen. As we cackled and sipped on our drink of choice, one of the dancers appeared out of nowhere. "So, how you ladies doin'?" he asked, beaming. No warmer smile had ever been intended for me as his had at that moment. Ever. His charm was undeniable and I was immediately smitten—quietly, of course. He made it a point to come over and introduce himself to me directly. "Hello, my name is Mr. Delight," he said, then smiled brightly. Like a bashful little girl I muttered a response and primped a smile right back at him. "What is your name?" he asked next. Without hesitation I rattled off everything but my social security number.

When intermission was over the stripper and the others went back to the stage for a lusty finale. The stripper seemed to dance now for me only, or so I wanted to believe. This time, when he exited the stage, he approached me, expressed an interest in getting to know me, then asked me out on a date and I accepted. I could not believe it! Julie had that I-told-you-so look on her face. "Now, see, coming out of the house got you a date and maybe a boyfriend too!"

Very quickly the stripper and I developed a steady relationship filled with affection and fun. I moved from the place I was living in when I first met him and together we moved to a slightly larger place that was more sustaining for two adults and two children. Equally, our time together consisted of long, lurid conversations. At times I felt like a therapist, then at times a mere sounding board; the stripper became a man of many words and terms describing his life and its downfalls. Like a little boy he would snuggle up to me and lay his head on my breasts or shoulder and talk. Yes, it was endless conversation. The pictures he painted of his father were that of abuse and resentment. He always expressed how he wanted to accomplish things in his life but was cheated out of the opportunities. "All I need is a good wife and I know I could get these things done," he'd say. "I would treat her so much better than my father treated my mother." However, somewhere in there, he loved his father and longed to have the storybook relationship with him that he'd always longed for. Compared to my family and upbringing, he definitely had it worse than I ever did. My heart went out to the stripper because for one, he was such a sweetheart, a charm to my heart. I believed he would never hurt a fly.

Just a few months into our relationship, the stripper wanted to get married. At twenty-seven and feeling like the opportunity might not come again, I said yes, why not. He'd proven enough to me. He was loving and charming; he respected me and my two daughters; he contributed financially. What more could a girl ask for?

Right there in the middle of the living room in our apartment, we exchanged vows before God and my brother, Rev. Anton Davis, who'd been the officiate.

A question that burns in my mind to this day was why was he crying so hard after the ceremony? I could tell those tears were not tears of joy. It was eerie. I remember standing there with a nervous half-cracked smile and a feeling of terror.

Talk about hoopla? There wasn't any. I'd borrowed a wedding gown from Julie's cousin and the stripper wore a linen suit as we went forth with the ceremony. My family was not present, but the stripper's father and two of his brothers were. The strange thing was this: the stripper's father's eyes burned a hole through me as he repeatedly commented, "Oh, you're so beautiful." His gaze was eerie. I hated it and wanted him to stop. If signs are supposed to give directions, I certainly failed to obey this one. Another thing I found strange was the presence at my wedding of two young ladies the stripper knew from the club. The stripper had invited them, which of course he'd had every right to. The problem was after the ceremony I'd overheard them tell the stripper in disgust, "I didn't believe you were going to marry her!" and "I can't believe you married her. You really married her!"

I frowned and figured they must've been jealous because they missed out. The truth was, however, they were two flames from the club where the stripper still worked as a stripper; he'd been fooling around with them. But, hey, our life went on. We were now Mr. and Mrs. Delite.

I had drifted away from church over the years, then later I attended various other churches and then drifted away again, finally returning to my first church, King David MBC.

We began to peek our heads in the door of the church and I never saw a man cry the way he cried. Every time we attended church, the stripper would cry like a baby. He'd just be wailing! I would say to myself, he must have finally found the spirit of God, not knowing it could have been guilt from things he had done or was thinking about doing.

The Cats

Remembering the many ways that I've been spared by God amazes me and brings tears to my eyes. People have always said that God works in mysterious ways. Well, listen, one day I was feeding stray cats as I'd always done. In fact I was called Cat Lady for my diligence in feeding them. The cats knew me well and would gather on the balcony in the front of my first floor apartment to wait for their food.

One day I was out talking to a neighbor from across the street. I was on one curb and he on the other; the two-way street divided us. As we laughed and talked, the conversation became engrossing, so I said, "Hey, wait a minute. I'm going to come on across the street." In my peripheral vision I could see some of the cats coming. As I approached the curb, I looked both ways to ensure no cars were coming—and there were absolutely no cars coming from either direction for as far as I could see. I stepped off the curb between two parked cars, and when I got a quarter of the-way across the street, a black car was suddenly screeching upon me. I was centered in front of the grill and I couldn't move forward or backward. I whispered to myself, *I'm dead* and all I could hear was my neighbor screaming, "Oh my God! Oh my God, she's dead."

At the same time as all of this was happening, my neighbor was so shocked and horrified at what he was seeing that he covered his face with his hands and fell to the ground while screaming, "Oh my God! Oh my God, she's dead!"

I don't know how, but the next vision I captured as I took my hands away from my face was cats all around me. Was I in heaven? No! I was alive and standing on the same sidewalk I had stepped off of, facing toward the street, away from my house! There were eight cats circled around me, all standing side by side, staring at me and not making a sound.

Once I gathered myself, still shaken, I stepped over the cats and then walked toward my apartment. The cats didn't move from their spot but turned their heads toward me, looking over their shoulders as I stepped over them and walked. Their stares followed me all the way to my home. They were my furry protectors. God seemed to always protect me through any means necessary, even through cats.

I never looked back at my neighbor across the street, but I could still hear him screaming, "That's impossible! How did you do that? How did you get back to the curb?" He just kept repeating those words. To this day I truly believe the devil was trying to kill me but God saved me. God has a purpose for me. Once again, can you see him?

The stripper and I had been living in this new building for a short time when one day I was coming home to my first floor apartment and a little girl who lived on the third floor, about eleven years old, ran down the stairs, pointed to my door and yelled to me, sobbing, "That man raped me!" The other neighbors in the building began coming out of their doors and looking. This was an alarm being sounded that upset everyone in my entire apartment building. I was equally, if not more, disturbed as she sobbed because *that man* was my husband she was accusing. I was furious and spouted, "What are you talking about?" At that moment my husband opened the door to our apartment and she repeated, pointing this time at my husband, "*That* man raped me." I thought to myself, *How and why would this little fast behind girl pick my husband to lie about?* There was no way the stripper, a gentle charmer, could do anything like that. *I have two little girls and they are perfectly safe with him and they adored him,* I pondered. *Oh, she's just a little trouble-making liar.*

My husband said to the girl, "What are you talking about?" and looking at me, said, "I was in the house! Why would she say something like that?" This went back and forth for some time while my neighbors were all looking at the scene. I was so shocked and embarrassed. In all fairness and in the midst of the uproar in our building, however, I went to the stripper and questioned him. "Why is that little girl saying you raped her? Surely you have not touched her, have you?"

"No! Of course not!" he squealed. "Why would I do that to a little girl, honey? Oh my God, I would never do such a thing to a child!" he insisted. He became angry and said, "We got two girls of our own! Why would you even ask me questions like that? How dare you!"

I believed him because that girl was one of those who was "mature for her age" or trying to be and was known for dressing suggestively for her age and flirting with older boys and even men in the neighborhood. My husband said, "She was always trying to get my attention and she's just mad at me because I would never pay any attention to her. You know how she runs back and forth, flirting with all the boys in the neighborhood." I said, "Okay, baby, I was just asking because she is insisting that you did that to her."

I felt like we had to build our ammunition for the fight, but instead we packed up and moved from that building and ended up living the furthest away that I'd ever lived from my immediate family. With two little girls, it was safe and convenient to live near my parents, however, being married now perhaps I was still safe and secure. Surely, I would find out *that* child was an alarm I didn't hear.

Life with the stripper was pretty regulated. He worked on and off as any stripper would, I guess. But my work was pretty steady, working at the juvenile court, filing cases and taking them to court.

I remember how I got that job: One day my girlfriend Julie invited me to a service at a certain church, not my normal church but a different church, and during the service there was an announcement that the presiding juvenile court judge was going to come up and talk about what was happening in the juvenile court system in the city of Chicago. He came up and talked about how we can keep our children safe, and after he spoke to the congregation, we decided to leave. It just so happens that he was leaving at the same time as we were, and we ran into him at the top of the church stairs. I told him how I liked and supported what he was doing in the community and the juvenile system, and he invited me to see the juvenile court building. I made an appointment with him and he gave me a tour of the juvenile building personally (that was nothing but God). After the tour, we went to his office. He asked me what I was doing for a living and I said I was looking for employment. He asked me if I would be interested in working for the juvenile system. I said yes, very much, and I was then hired to file cases and take them to court and I also worked on the information desk. I worked with all the judges. This was the highest position you could get as a non-college graduate. I once heard my new supervisor make a comment. "She must be a spy because nobody gets hired with the court system like she was and get a position like this." I know now it was nothing but divine favor.

During my time with the juvenile system, I met a lady whose name was Venus. Venus and I became good friends. In fact she lived around the corner from me. Venus came to me one day and said "Every year some of the employees put on a show for the juvenile court system and one of our fellow employees, I'll call him Mike, was looking for dancers to be in the show in which they were going to do Michael Jackson's Thriller. I loved being on stage and I thought it would be really fun so I agreed to do it.

We rehearsed night after night after night. But oh what a good time we had preparing for this show. The costumes, doing makeup, I was doing what I loved the most— entertaining. There were two shows at the courthouse and they turned out so well that an additional show was requested at another location.

At the first show, my parents, the Stripper and my two daughters were there and they loved it. Who wouldn't love Thriller performed to perfection – we knew every step, every movement and every gesture. I remember Venus always used to walk down the hall at the juvenile court doing the Thriller steps. She was such a wonderful person. I really loved her.

I remember one day I was at work and the stripper drove up to my office, came in and said, "I kept Sharron [my youngest daughter] home from school today because she's looking bad. She's in the car and I think you better have a look at her." When I went to the car and saw her, horror filled my face. She looked terrible! I yelled at the stripper, saying, "Why did you bring her here? Why didn't you take her to the hospital?"

He said, "I didn't know what else to do, so I brought her here." He said, "She's been throwing up, didn't want to get out of bed, and she just wasn't looking right." From the way she looked, I knew we had to take her to the hospital.

Grabbing my coat and purse, I yelled to my supervisor, "I'm taking my daughter to the hospital. She's outside in the car and she's very sick." The stripper and I immediately took her there.

Once we were there, they took one look at her, took her from us, put her in a wheelchair, and made us wait in a waiting area. A half an hour later they came to us and told us they took her to ICU and made us put on masks and gowns before we could visit her. The doctor came into the room and told us that she was critically ill. She had a disease called meningetis. He said it's a very serious disease and we'll know within the next twenty-four hours if she is going to survive it. I cried all the way to the hospital chapel where I went and prayed to God that he would heal her from this disease and bring her back to me. It was two days later that we were told that not only would she survive but she would live without any permanent damage to her system. They also told me that if we didn't get her to the hospital when we did, she would have died. Glory be to God! At the time I didn't realize it was His grace and mercy that brought her through, but in my mind I thought it was the stripper that saved her. Because of that thought, after that, I trusted the stripper implicitly—he could now do no wrong. But it was really God and God alone who saved her. To God be the glory!

In addition to my job I added volunteer work, which I loved. In the year that Harold Washington was running to be the first elected black mayor of Chicago, I was all over it. I volunteered in the evenings after work, which meant that the stripper was Mr. Mom for a while. We'd been married two years now; we were indeed family. He was good with my girls—or so I thought. He cooked, saw to their homework, and tucked them in at night if I had not gotten home by bedtime. I would soon find out what *good* really meant however.

My girls were my everything. They were normal little girls with imagination and a love for cartoons and certain television shows. My oldest daughter in particular loved *Little House on the Prairie*. The father image was what grasped her interest the most and stirred her own desire for such a father. He was anything but, but she had hopes.

The Stripper's Father

The stripper's father's visits had become quite frequent and I remember how he always wanted to treat us, especially the girls. He'd give me money and tell me to go to the store and buy goodies for myself and the girls. Whenever I'd go on these errands, I always felt an urgency like I had to get back as soon as possible. Even though he always acted like the nicest gentleman, I couldn't help feeling a certain unease. I remember once when I came back from one of these errands, for some reason my spirit had me walking quietly like a cat, like I was trying to catch him at something. He was sitting on my daughter's bed while she was in bed. It seemed like he didn't notice me there, and then suddenly realized I was there, and so he quickly picked up a book and opened it like he was pretending to read it to my daughter. It was years later when I found that the unease in my spirit about him was right. I found out that one day he took my daughter to the store and while she was sitting in the passenger side of the car, he started rubbing her thigh. She started crying, saying, "Stop it—I don't like that. I'm telling my mom." He then pulled his hand back and said, "My God! What am I doing?" After that he stopped coming around much anymore. At the time I always wondered why he stopped coming around and it was years later before I found out why.

While Harold Washington's campaign was jumping off with all the success imaginable, I was proud and fulfilled, working it and thinking my kids were home safe, warm, and filled. But I didn't know just how filled they were.

It was years later when I found out that on one of the many nights while I was working and campaigning, the stripper sent my daughter on a short errand there in the apartment to retrieve a towel for him. She did so and when she presented it to him, he told her to spread it out on the bed and get on top of it. My youngest daughter was also in the bed in the first position. He told her to lay on the towel in the middle and, being the so-called gentle charmer that he was, he snuggled behind her first and convinced her it was like the father in *Little House on the Prairie*. Initially, in her young mind, my daughter thought this was a dream come true, a father who loves affectionately and safely. That is how the stripper penetrated the door of my baby's trust, literally. He raped her.

The stripper became the murderer of my daughter's soul as he repeated his lustful behavior toward her for quite some time. I only found out about this many years later through a psychiatrist after my daughter attempted suicide. Many hints fluttered before me, but I didn't get it. Wake up, ladies! Are your daughters or sons safe? Are there signs all around you that you don't see?

What I haven't said though, is that the stripper was beginning to slap me around a bit as it was. Regardless, I didn't think he would harm my daughters in any way. How wrong I was. Many times things go on among adults and we think we are doing a thorough job of hiding from our kids, but my daughters knew the stripper was beating me and my oldest daughter felt obligated to protect her younger sister and me, so she took the abuse as the stripper told her, "If you tell, I will kill your mother and rape your sister too."

Rape violates you both sexually and emotionally. It is a sexual act of violence. It is sex without consent. It is a sin. Some of the myths about rape are that the victim likes it, that it fulfils their sexual needs, or that dressing provocatively causes it. But the truth is rape is not about sex because sex is an act of love between a husband and his wife. Rape and sex are opposites. Sex without consent is rape. Regardless of how a person dresses, nobody desires to be raped.

I took a couple of days off from work and while the kids were at school and the stripper was out, the doorbell rang. It was a woman with her two kids and she asked if Delite was home. I said, "No, he isn't, but I am."

She said, "Who are you?"

"I'm his wife," I said.

She said, "He ain't got no wife!"

I corrected her grammar. "It's not 'He ain't got no wife,' it's 'He don't have a wife,' and yes, he does have a wife because I'm his wife." I then heard her say something smart and I yelled, "You stay right there!" and I immediately jumped up and ran down the stairs to have it out with her. As I got out the front door, I saw her shove her kids into a car, jump into the front seat, slamming the door as she cussed me out and sped off. She didn't realize she wasn't a girlfriend, she was just a victim with kids—but this time the kids were a girl *and* a boy. Months later she would also find out who he really was because he moved in with her and I moved into another apartment.

Bruce

Our marital bliss was filled with increasing turmoil as months passed. The stripper continued stripping at the club where I'd first met him. His deceptive charm and inviting smile became a latch hook that would create new relationships that brought even more changes and complications to our marriage. There was already the secret that he was molesting my daughter. Mine and the stripper's roles gradually switched. I was home in the evenings and he was out working. He would get home later and later. I'll never forget the first night he came home from work in the wee hours with a male friend.
"Who is that?
"Baby, this is my friend Bruce," said the stripper
"Okay, well, why do you have him here so late?
"Well, come here. Let me show you."
"Stop playing. Show me what?"
The stripper, Bruce and I went to an area in the kitchen where they pulled out drugs and all the paraphernalia that went with it. Of course I had done some marijuana and I liked my drinks, but this didn't look at all familiar. They took a test tube, put cocaine in it and added a couple drops of water. Then they took a broken end of a coat hanger with a cotton swab on the end, dipped the hanger in some grain alcohol, and lit the cotton swab under the tube until it began to boil. Then they took another piece of the broken hanger and put it in the tube and stirred it until all the liquefied cocaine clinged to the hanger and gently pulled it out so none of the substance touched the side of the tube and placed it on a mirror. Within thirty seconds it hardened and they scraped all the cocaine off the end of the hanger with a razor blade. Then they placed it into a cocaine pipe and dipped the cotton swab again into some grain alcohol and packed it tight into the glass pipe. When I saw this my eyes got really big. *What the heck is that?* I wondered. Bruce put the pipe to his mouth, clamped down with his lips wrapped

around the tip and sucked in hard, collapsing his cheeks. He inhaled all the smoke into his lungs and held it, then exhaled slowly. His eyes immediately popped wide open, and for a moment he just stared into space and didn't speak at all. You could actually see his heart racing through his tee shirt. Then he said, "Wow! That was a good hit!" I sat there speechless. His wide stares and silence scared me. (This is how they smoked cocaine before rocks came out.) My husband was busy working on his concoction and took a look at me before doing what Bruce had just done.

"Come on, baby, try it. It'll make you feel good," he said to me. It felt welcoming that my husband was including me and it was, after all, something we could do together.

Another thing that prompted me to try it was when I saw my husband and Bruce do a "shotgun." What they did was Bruce went through the same procedure again holding the smoke in his mouth, pressed his lips to my husband's lips and blew the smoke into my husband's mouth. I thought to myself, *Oh no—if anyone's gonna kiss my husband it's gonna be me!*

"Okay, what do I do first?" I asked.

"Let me help you, baby," my husband gently offered. He took some of the cocaine off the mirror and put it into the glass pipe and dipped the cotton into the grain alcohol, lit it over the pipe, and said, "When you see the smoke, slowly inhale until you can't inhale anymore, and then hold it as long as you can and then slowly release it."

Once I released the smoke, I cried, "Oh my God! Something must be wrong! I'm having a heart attack!"

He said "Relax! Relax! Breathe slow and enjoy the hit!"

My heart was beating so fast I thought I was going to die. My husband and Bruce looked at each other and turned to me and said, "That's the high. That's the best hit you'll ever get in your life." This would become the new Friday night ritual in our home. My husband held my hand as he lured me into a world of crack cocaine, almost the death of me.

To look at my husband, one would not dub him as the drug using kind. He was clean cut, slender, well built, and tall.

His skin color was much lighter than my dark chocolate skin, and he had a kind face at all times. This well-groomed but problematic "gentleman" and husband would spend his entire paycheck on this new vice. It had become sheer joy for him. He and Bruce became inseparable as friends and fellow drug users. They were thrilled that I had joined them and they had a place to go where they didn't have to sneak or hurry or explain what happened to the paycheck. This was my house, the place where I was supposed to responsibly raise my girls and live as a good wife to my husband. In short it had now become a crack house.

My husband and Bruce seemed to be growing into more of a couple than he and I was. The two of them spent time together on and off crack cocaine, but the drug, I believe, was the glue that held them together, not to speak of the fact that our place was now their place for using. Furthermore, I was now looking forward to them coming home every Friday so that we could do the drug together officially. Every Friday I would anxiously put the girls to bed early. Now that we lived near the "L," it was very convenient for me to look intently out the window, waiting to see them get off the train. Believe it or not, it wasn't the drug I preferred, it was simply being with my husband and being accepted by his friend. That was the reason I would smoke the crack every time.

This new life of doing drugs right on the other side of the door where my children slept was becoming menacing for sure, but I did not want to be left out of the loop. However, eventually, that is exactly what happened. One Friday night, the stripper and Bruce just didn't show up, then the next Friday and finally the next Friday. No husband, no drugs, no Bruce. It turns out they'd started going somewhere else to use without me. I felt so left out. But now I had a new problem. I wanted the drug.

At that time my worst fear was that my husband's and Bruce's involvement with each other was more than just drug related. I remembered back on several occasions when they were at our place that their "shotguns" were lasting longer and longer. I asked myself, *Why were they even giving each other 'shotguns' in the first place?* I worried that my husband was becoming more attracted to Bruce than to me—and I was right. I later found out he was bisexual.

My life with the stripper was like a perpetual descending spiral. As a result, my head spun even when I was standing still; my heart hurt for his obvious infidelities.

His disappearing acts had become continuous as he'd literally pack up and move out of our apartment to live with another woman for weeks at a time, and all I could guess was they had something I surely did not. Remember the woman with the two kids that came to my door? I wondered what she had that I didn't. The latest in technology, like a VCR, perhaps? Maybe they could have sex standing on their heads? Maybe they had free drugs too.

I knew my husband was a fiend for crack, but one good thing about this situation was it took me away from crack—at least for now.

Enter the Drug Dealer

When I spoke of divorce, he disputed it as if we had too much to lose. He whined like a child and declared his love for me and only me. He tried desperately to convince me that he could not live without me. Regardless, this rotating spiral that had bore through the world of Mr. and Mrs. Delite finally halted in Hell, and I got off after three years of demented riding. We were formally separated.

As a previously addicted single mother, I rambled on. Thank God I was still highly functional because there was no doubt I had to make a living for my girls and me, so off to work I went in a blur of odd jobs. A juggling act of real life needs, my taste for drugs, and the wellbeing of my girls was now my reason for existence that I fumbled along in. My parents and siblings were very concerned about me but didn't know any details, and of course I was not telling.

After leaving the stripper, I stopped using cocaine, but I still found my comfort in smoking marijuana. Drug suppliers in Chicago were a penny a dozen, so finding one was no problem at all, which I did. In fact one day, when I had gone to my new supplier's house to get some marijuana from him, I was so focused on my mission I really hadn't looked at him through wandering eyes at all. I just wanted to get my weed and split. I was done with crack. One day my girlfriend, who was a former coworker at the candy company with me and who lived in the apartment across from me, told me I had to get out of the house some and invited me out to a party that night. At first I declined, but she kept asking me. Eventually I agreed to go, found a babysitter, and went with her. (Doesn't that sound familiar?) That's when I had the opportunity to talk to the drug dealer. I found out when I got to the party that it was for his birthday.

It was at his sister's house and there were a lot of people there waiting in a line to greet him. When he got to me, I put out my hand as for a handshake and he said, "You can do better than that" and gave me a big hug with a big smile on his face. I thought he looked really sharp. He had a perfect Jheri curl and was wearing the sharpest suit I'd ever seen with a matching tie and shoes. He seemed humble and very soft-spoken. I was both attracted to him and afraid because of what men had just done to me before—but he was CUTE! He didn't take his eyes off of me the whole night. I didn't know this at the time but his wife, who he was separated from, was also there and also noticed he couldn't keep his eyes off of me.

Eventually, his wife went downstairs, and when a slow record came on he saw his chance and eased on over to me, and he politely asked me to dance. We danced for several records.

After several dances, I decided I needed to go home and be with my girls, and so I headed down the stairs with him following me down as though he wanted to walk me home. Behind, this woman I didn't know followed him and said, "Where do you think you're going?" He looked at me and then at her with a frustrated look on his face. I then disappeared into the night. I later found out the woman behind him on the stairs was his wife. It was like a Cinderella story where I, the princess, had to run off, leaving the prince behind. He was certainly one of the most desired men in the neighborhood: he was well mannered, well dressed, available and, due to his business, had money. It was a number of weeks before I saw him again.

The next time I saw him, I met him at his spot to buy some marijuana. He was an avid chess player and was playing chess. As I made my purchase, he asked if he could come and visit me some time. I said, "Sure. Why not." And that night, he showed up at my door.

The drug dealer and I started seeing each other quite regularly now, and I no longer called the stripper or even answered his calls. I eventually called the stripper and he started telling me how he missed me, how he wanted to get back together, and how he wanted to work things out. He said he was going to be such a good husband from now on. I asked, "Do you really want to work things out?"

He said "Yes, I do." So I said come on over. What I didn't say was the drug dealer gave me money to go to the courthouse and get divorce papers for him to sign. When the stripper got to my place, he didn't know we weren't alone. He expected me to run to him with open arms and tell him how I loved him and wanted to work things out. When he stepped into my apartment, I immediately locked the door behind him so he and I were standing in my hallway. He knew by the expression on my face and my manner that this meeting wasn't going to be what he expected. He said, "What's going on?"

I said, "I got these papers I want you to sign."

"What papers?"

"Divorce papers."

With that he resentfully said, "I ain't signin' no damn divorce papers!" He began to step toward me in an aggressive manner but then as he did so, he noticed the drug dealer come out from the bedroom and then my brother step out from the living room. The three of us encircled him, surrounding him. The stripper's aggressive manner suddenly disappeared. Speaking to the drug dealer, the stripper said, "Hey, man, who are you?"

The drug dealer said, "That's my woman you talkin' to, and I don't like the way you're talkin' to my woman!"

The stripper said, "Man, that's my wife!"

"That WAS your wife. Sign these papers!"

The stripper looked at me, then nervously at the drug dealer and then my brother. The stripper knew he was trapped and wasn't getting out of my apartment until he signed the papers, so he signed them and left. As soon as he left, he made his way to the first pay phone he found and called me and said, "What did you do? You set me up!" And that, folks, was the end of the stripper!

Soon after the divorce from the stripper was finalized, the drug dealer asked me to marry him and I gladly said yes.

The wedding was going to be at 3:00 p.m. in my apartment with my brother, the preacher who was going to perform the ceremony. The drug dealer went out for a bachelor party the night before and I didn't see or hear from him the morning of the wedding. I called his friend, who was a barber and his best man. "Where is he?" I asked.

"He's sleeping. I'll wake him when I'm done working."

I was frantic and furious. "You need to wake him now! We're getting married at three!"

His friend insisted, "I'll wake him when I'm done working. Don't worry. We'll be there on time." At 1:00 p.m, I couldn't reach him and I was so freaked out and angry I didn't know what to do. He finally showed up about an hour before the ceremony and apologized profusely. Things finally calmed down and the wedding proceeded normally. The dress my mother bought me was a pink lace dress, white lace stockings, and pink shoes. The hat I wore was pink and had a white lace veil. It was beautiful. When I walked along the long hallway of the apartment and made it to the living room where the wedding was presiding, the ooohs and ahhs filled the room. When I saw the bridegroom, his eyes lit up with love as I entered. An amazing thing happened next. We were holding hands during the vows, and I felt my spirit step out of my body and into his.

I could feel first one foot step out of my body and into his and then I could feel the other foot step out of my body and into his and then finally the rest of my body entered his. I could then feel his first leg step into my body, his other leg and then the rest of his body step into mine. My eyes were wide and I looked at his face, and his eyes were also wide like he was feeling the same thing I was. I knew we were soulmates. After the wedding I described what I felt and he said, "Yeah! I felt it too!" And we both said together, "We're soulmates! We're soulmates!" I have never felt this before or since with any of my other husbands. Furthermore no person I have ever talked to has said they felt anything like it either. He was clearly my soulmate.

Ultimately, my drug supplier became my husband and the comfort I needed to get over the devastation that the stripper had brought to my life. At that time, the good thing was my husband only dealt marijuana, not crack. This was good because, like I said, crack was not what I preferred anyway, it just had that unyielding grip I thought I'd never be free of. My drug of choice was indeed marijuana. The drug dealer and I got along great and immediately went into "business" together successfully. We had a clientele miles long and I, and my girls, wanted for nothing.

We were happily married and on our way. We first lived in a second floor apartment and when the first floor apartment became available, we rented that one too.

That one would be the one we'd call our spot for business. We dealt and sold marijuana from that first floor apartment for quite a while. We kept the building clean, we had lookouts keeping the building secure, and we bought food and gifts for both my family and everyone else in the building. Everyone in the building was one big happy family, except for the building handyman. He was always bad mouthing us to the owner of the building because he was jealous. But the owner saw how well we took care of the building and how safe and secure it was for the tenants, so he had no problem with us.

The ill-gotten gains of the drug trade seemed mind bogglingly limitless. At the time I really thought I hit the jackpot, marrying my drug dealer husband, because of the extravagant material luxury he could afford. We'd rent limo rides just to drive around the city for fun. We'd have weekly getaways to the best room at the Ritz Carlton in downtown Chicago. He even sent my children to Hawaii for a month to stay with my brother and his wife who lived there. My drug dealer husband would provide me and my daughters anything our hearts desired. I remember the drug dealer's bootleg friends would come over, I would tell them what I wanted—be it designer clothes, luxury furniture, anything—and they would steal it from the best stores in town. I only wanted the best name brand merchandise and they got it for me.

The Killer Nurse

At the age of nine years old I started menstruation. I was such a little bitty thing and I was always a heavy bleeder and a heavy, heavy cramper. By the time I reached thirty I had been heavily bleeding and cramping for twenty-one years. I couldn't take it any longer. My bleeding went from one week per month to two. I went to the doctor and found out I had a fibroid tumor. After some tests, I was told it wasn't going to get any better. The tumor was only going to grow and the bleeding and cramping would get worse. When I heard this, I decided to have a hysterectomy.

I was put in the hospital and before the surgery, the doctor told me that sometimes an infection could be associated with this operation, but it would be highly unlikely. So, of course, I got a very serious infection—serious enough to be put in the ICU. In ICU, I gradually became aware of my surroundings. I couldn't tell whether it was day or night because the room had no windows and I couldn't tell what time it was because there was no clock on any wall I could see. Because of these conditions, I couldn't tell how long I was there, but I felt it was more than twenty-four hours. I was actually there for three days. When I became fully conscious, the doctor told me the tumor was the size of a large orange. I asked the nurse if my family could visit me or if I could call my family. I was told I could see no one yet, and I accepted this at first. When I recovered enough to move around, they stood me up and had me walk as part of my recovery. The nurse I had for this was an extremely mean-tempered one who was unnecessarily rough when she stood me up and bodily pushed me to force me to walk up and down the hall. I told her I was in a lot of pain and didn't feel well enough to walk and asked her to be more gentle with me. Her response was a barrage of profanity and even rougher handling as she bodily pushed me down the hall. She would do this every day. I thought to myself, *Is she the only nurse around here?* It was then I noticed there was no other staff in the entire ICU. I thought to myself, *Where is all the other staff?* I later noticed that there were no other patients in that ICU either—it was just her and me.

One day, she finally took a twenty-minute break and another nurse came into my room. I told her what the other nurse was like and what she was doing to me and asked, "When can my family visit me?" She told me my folks were downstairs and they had tried to visit me for the past few days, but the mean nurse told them I was too sick to see anyone. The new nurse said she thought I was well enough to see my family but instructed me that they could only see me for five minutes, and then they had to leave. She told me, "Please don't tell the other nurse you had visitors!" It was as if she was afraid of the mean nurse or what that nurse might do. As it turns out, my mean nurse was the head nurse. The nice nurse snuck my family in to visit me, and I told them what was going on. I pleaded with them, "You got to get me out of here!"

When the evil nurse came back, I gave her a piece my mind, saying, "I saw my family! My family is going to get me out of here! You can't keep me here!"

She menacingly said, "You're not getting out of here! You're not *ever* getting out of here! The only way you're getting out of here is through the morgue!" I wasn't afraid because she was a nurse. I didn't think she would really try to kill me. I just thought she was trying to scare me. From then on I felt "It's on chicken-bone!" between her and me. She tormented me all that night.

The next day, she stepped out of my room for a while and I saw my opportunity to sneak a few puffs of a cigarette in the bathroom. When she came back, she smelled the cigarette smoke, caught me in the bathroom, and roughly pushed me back into bed. Now she really went off on me with profanity, how I was never going to get out of here, and how I was going to die. I was so scared I started hyperventilating, and as I was hyperventilating, the evil nurse continued screaming profanity at me and said, "Yeah! Hyperventilate! Yeah! Hyperventilate," and, "You're gonna die! You're gonna die!" While she was screaming this at me, she started to disconnect my oxygen, but before she could finish, doctors, nurses, and all kinds of staff appeared out of nowhere and violently pushed the evil nurse out of the way. The doctors put a bag over my head and said, "Breathe slow! Breathe slow!" Once they got me stable, I heard instructions to move me downstairs to a different room. I couldn't understand where all those medical staff came from out of nowhere but I thanked God for them! Can you see God now?

The room they moved me to was on the floor below, in a regular patient room with another female patient, a window, and a phone. My bed was near the window and not the door. I was surprised they put me in a normal room because I thought I was maybe too sick yet, but nonetheless I was glad to get away from that ICU and that nurse—or so I thought. That night, I saw the evil nurse walking back and forth past my door. She was watching me! Something told me not to go to sleep or else I may not ever wake up again because of her. So I watched her as she watched me as she walked past my door all night long.

The following day, they hurriedly discharged me and sent me home. Once again, I was surprised they discharged me this early because I was still very sick, but I thanked God I was out of there! It wasn't until later that I understood why the staff suddenly appeared in ICU when I was hyperventilating, why they moved me into a regular room with another patient, and why I was suddenly discharged the next day even though I was still sick.

About a couple of days after being discharged, two orderlies from the hospital came to my home and told my husband they wanted to see me and had something to tell me. He let them in and they told me why they came. They said they were happily surprised at how lucky I was to get out of that hospital alive. They said that many patients in that ICU under that nurse's care never made it out alive. Patients would come in for fairly minor procedures and then die under her care. This happened too many times to be coincidence and they were sure she was causing the patients deaths. She was killing patients, they knew she was after me, and they were sure she was going to get me! And that is why they released me in the state I was in.

I realized then that I was bait in some kind of sting operation on the evil nurse. The staff was hiding on the sidelines until the evil nurse made her move to finish me off! When they caught her in the act of trying to unplug my oxygen, they pounced on her and saved my life.

I also realized then that God was looking out for me! He saved my life! If it wasn't for the angel God had sent in between those twenty minutes where the other nurse came in, I would never have gotten my word out what the evil nurse was doing to me and that I wanted to get out. If it wasn't for the staff suddenly appearing from nowhere, I might have died at the hands of that killer nurse! If it wasn't for the Lord delivering me from the hands of the evil nurse, I would have died for sure. Do you see him? She was soon fired—but where did she go? I felt guilty for a long time about not doing more to follow up on her, because who's next? Now, there are two kinds of guilt: good guilt makes us stop doing destructive things and change our ways to improve our lives. Bad guilt makes us dwell on our weaknesses and failures and brings us down. This is not the first or last time I would feel the bad guilt from satan.

The Raid

I remember one day, I was at home cooking a seven-course meal like I always did. I cooked greens, chicken with gravy and rice, macaroni and cheese, sweet potatoes, corn bread, and banana pudding. I had just put the banana pudding in the oven to brown the egg white, when all of a sudden I heard a loud BOOM! Then I heard it again. My daughters had invited the neighbor's kids over to play and everyone was running around when we heard that noise. We thought we were being stuck up, and so I told the kids to go in the back room. We heard another loud BOOM, and with that the door flew open and in rushed a bunch of police. The first ones in were plainclothes police (my daughters thought they were the stick up men and we were all going to die). They gathered everyone up and made us all lay down on our stomachs on the kitchen floor. They made the kids lie under the table. The kids were screaming for dear life. All I could hear was loud voices shouting, "Where are the guns? Where are the drugs?"

I then politely asked, "Could I please take the banana pudding out of the oven?"

The police sergeant said, "Sure." The raid happened so fast that we had no time to hide any drugs, and so some were sitting right out on the kitchen table. The police said, "There's some drugs!" pointing out the drugs laying on the table. The police put a gun to my husband's head and shouted at my husband, "Where's the guns?"

My husband said, "It's in the room." Some time ago my husband bought me a four-barrel .357 magnum with hollow point bullets for just in case someone attacked us—and I knew how to use guns because every New Year's Eve, my father would have us all load and fire his .32 caliber pistol. He would show us how to load and unload it, as well as flip the safety on and off. I had hidden the gun in the headboard of my bed. The police kept demanding to see the gun, so I took them into the bedroom and opened the headboard, revealing the gun. It wasn't obvious the headboard opened, so it was like a secret compartment. The police commented that it was a very clever hiding place. They admitted, "We would never have found it on our own." On the way back to the kitchen with the gun, I heard a cop screaming and saw him running from the girls bedroom and back into the kitchen. He yelled, "There's something in there! There's something in there!" So they eased on into the room with guns drawn, and all of a sudden they saw two eyes glowing in the dark. When they turned the light on, they saw a three-foot-tall toy robot that would come to life when it heard a sound. Everyone was laughing hysterically—which took off some of the tension on everyone. After they discovered the robot, they began to notice all the other nice things we got for the kids and were impressed at how well we took care of them and how well mannered we were. That's when the police sergeant said, "I like y'all. You're house is clean and neat, the furniture is beautiful, the kids have everything they could ask for, the pantry is full of food, you're cooking a beautiful dinner for your kids. We never busted any drug dealers like y'all." In fact, when some of the other officers wanted to tear up the pantry looking for drugs, the sergeant said, "Hey don't mess up the pantry! There ain't nothin' in that pantry. Look at how neatly stacked those cans are." At this time the police told the kids to go to a neighbor's house, and after the kids left, asked whose gun and whose drugs they were. Beforehand we had planned for my brother to say the gun was his because he had never been in trouble before, and if they knew it was the drug dealer's, he could do some serious jail time because of his prior record. If that happened, that would have stopped our livelihood. Again, the police asked whose gun it was. My brother said nothing, so I said it was mine out of loyalty to my husband (what a dumb thing for me to do). My brother then said it was his too. My husband and I glared at my brother, since now there would be two people to bail out of jail.

Finally, the police sergeant said we could get up and sit on the kitchen chairs. After that, the police decided I had to go to the station, but they were debating with each other about which officers were going to take me. The police that were there consisted of a sergeant, who was black, another black officer, and two white officers. By that time I had formed a relationship with the sergeant. However, the white officers insisted they take me to the station.

They put me in tight handcuffs and led me out the door and to the police car. All along the way the children and all of my neighbors were watching. I felt so humiliated. My children were crying all along the way. "Please don't take my mama away!" Something made me suspicious of the handyman, who also was witnessing this, because as they led me away, he said, "Why are you taking her? You should be taking him [my husband], not her." I think he liked me, but it was known he didn't like the drug dealer, and I think he was the one who tipped off the police about our operation. I think he called them on us because the police said, "We were watching you for long time and our informants have been buying from you all the time. We know you sell good stuff because if you weren't, we would have busted you a long time ago."

Once I arrived at the station, they put my brother and I in a small holding cell while they wrote out their report. My brother and I were talking, and some of the officers there said, "They're plotting something! We need to separate them!" So then the sergeant allowed me to sit at his desk. While I was sitting there, he explained that the reason they were debating on who was going to take me to the station was because if the black officers took me, they were going to drive a couple blocks away and let me go. The sergeant also expressed how well-furnished and ordered my apartment was—how the kids seemed well cared for and well fed. He said he'd never seen such a well provided for family on any of his busts. You see, on most of their busts, the houses were filthy with little or no food, neglected children with nothing on but dirty diapers, and unconscious drug users laying around. He said we were the nicest drug dealers they ever met. Then the sergeant asked me if I was hungry or if he could get me any soda from the vending machine. After that, we were kept overnight and slept on one of the coldest, hardest benches I ever experienced. I knew then I couldn't do this anymore. The next day my drug dealer husband bailed my brother and I out. He always bragged about that but I said, "Sure, you bailed us out, but we were protecting you! After all, all that money you earned wasn't just spent on me and my kids!" Two weeks later, we went to court and it was thrown out because the only thing that made it to court was three bags of marijuana and no gun.

A Man Came Up Behind Me

One night, the drug dealer and I went out to a bar where my girlfriend Debra worked as a barmaid. Debra grew up with me, and two of my brothers ended up marrying two of her sisters. The brother that lived with me and also went to jail with me married one of her sisters and my oldest brother Lamont, who you'll be hearing about later, married, her other sister. During the evening, the drug dealer and I got into an argument and he left the bar—leaving me sitting there, alone. I lived about a mile away from the bar and had to walk home alone after the bar closed. When I got to the front door of the house, a man came up behind me and I felt a gun pressing up against me. He took me to the basement entrance at the back of the building, and that's where he raped me. I was terrified, but I acted like I enjoyed it so he wouldn't kill me. After returning upstairs to my apartment, shaking, I called the police, and they took me to the hospital to have me checked out. The next day I received a phone call in which the caller said, "I saw what happened to you last night," and then hung up. I was angry and disappointed that someone could witness something so horrific and not call the police. It had to be someone I knew because they had to have my phone number to call me.

A week later the police came to my house and told me they had the man they believed had been raping women in the Austin area of Chicago, and maybe I could come with them to identify him in a lineup. I said it was pitch-black out and I never saw his face. They continued to try talking me into going with them for a lineup. "If nothing else, maybe you can identify him by the sound of his voice or some other feature." Seeing I was still hesitant, they told me about a fund for rape victims. I still didn't want to go and pick out the wrong man because I really couldn't be sure who it was. It was someone I never met before (at least I thought). When the police described their suspect, that was when I found out he was known as the "West Side Rapist." I never heard anything more about it.

Happy Marriage Fading

Because of our success, our apartment was always filled with people buying marijuana, hanging out, family, friends. We never seemed to have any time for each other. So many women would come through our home, many of them trying to get my husband's attentions, and likewise, a number of men would come through our home, trying to gain my attentions.

It got to the point where we started arguing, and eventually we argued a lot. Our happy little marriage began to fade away.

Spike

One day this man came to the apartment with some puppies. He told us his dog had puppies and he was selling them. There was this caramel-colored one that was the cutest little pit bull puppy I had ever seen. Usually pit bulls look kind of scary, but this puppy was not scary looking at all. My girls and I begged my husband to buy him, and so he did. We named him Spike and my girls and I loved that dog. As he was growing, our apartment became small for him; he was such a huge pit bull—such a gentle giant.

Spike was a shoe chewer, but he only chewed on mine and no one else's. I thought that dog hated me, until one day, my husband and I had a heated argument, and he threw me on the bed and started choking me. Spike immediately clamped his jaws down onto one of his feet. If my husband wasn't wearing shoes, that dog would have bit his foot off.

Spike had him by the foot and Jackie the cat had him by the head. They were protecting me! I love animals, and they've played important roles in my life.

Eventually my husband let me go and ran out the house. He called me back and apologized profusely, saying, "I'm so sorry. Can I come home? You're not gonna let your dog and cat get me are you?" That's how I found out that Spike really did love me after all. I thought to myself, *That dog can chew up my shoes as much as he wants.*

When he came back into the house, he acted all apologetic to everyone: me, the dog, the cat. He'd try to gently pet them, but they wouldn't have anything to do with him like they were suspicious of him—like I should have been.

A little while later, he said he'd like to take the dog for a walk. When he tried to put the leash on him, Spike didn't want to go. I told Spike to go on and let my husband put the leash on him, and he finally obeyed and they walked out the door. An hour or so later, here my husband comes in with this sad, dumb expression on his face with the leash in his hand. I said, "Where is Spike?" He didn't say anything. I said it again a little louder. "Where is Spike?"

"Aw. I got bad news. Spike was trying to chase a dog across the street and he got away from me and ran into a city bus. He was hit and his eyes popped out and he died." Now, why did he have to say "his eyes popped out"? He made it worse by saying that. My daughters and I screamed when he said that. He said, "I'm sorry, I didn't mean it. If you don't believe me, go outside and look."

I told him, "I do not want to go out and see him with his eyes popped out in the street! If you don't go out and get that dog and give him a decent burial, you can leave out this house!" It was weeks before my daughters would speak to him. I have always been suspicious about what happened—especially seeing him with that leash when he came through the door. Our cat Jackie was suspicious of him from then on. She wouldn't let him come near her or my girls or I without objecting. What do *you* think happened to Spike?

Nan

One night we had just come back from a night out at the Ritz Carlton in downtown Chicago, where we frequently visited to get away from it all. When we pulled up to our building, we saw an ambulance and police everywhere. We were afraid to go into our building. One of the neighbors in the building told me Nan, our mutual neighbor, had died. She had five children, two of which were girls that were about the same age as my girls, and they used to play together. (Those two girls were playing at our house when the raid happened.) They were like family. I was told Nan was found with the Bible open on her chest. She had died sometime that night while reading the Bible. It was a big shock to the whole building. I knew her children would have to be split up and placed in foster homes. I came *that* close to taking her children, but I'm glad I didn't for reasons that will be apparent later on.

What made it especially sad was that she was the "Christian of the building," the only one in the building who was routinely praying and studying the word. Now she was gone. I should have known then it was time to go.

Jackie and the Burglar

Jackie was an amazing cat. She even identified a burglar: the drug dealer and I went away overnight and when we returned the window above our apartment door was broken out, and Jackie was laying in that window frame, crying. When we went in, we could see that our house was carefully searched. No drawers were pulled out onto the floor; my minks were still there. My jewelry was carefully picked through. Some marijuana was taken, but bags of it were still there. No burglar in the world would have left what was left behind. The neat manner in which our house was searched told us it was an inside job. There were six apartments in our building, but when we talked to all of our neighbors, nobody said they heard anything. All this time, Jackie was acting like something was bothering her. I thought to myself, *Something is wrong with Jackie. I have to find out what's wrong with that cat. I've never seen her so anxious.* The last time I saw her that upset was when Spike died. I asked Jackie, "What's wrong? Do you know who broke into our house? Show me." And with that, Jackie started running around in circles, meowing loudly and acting even more distressed.

Later that evening our neighbor, the building's handyman, came to our apartment because we called him to repair the damage from the break-in and find out if maybe he heard anything about it. When I opened the door, the cat went ballistic. I never saw a cat act so agitated. In fact, we had to lock the cat up. The handyman looked startled—scared to death—and wouldn't set foot in the apartment. He said, "What's wrong with your cat? That cat is crazy! Why is your cat acting like that?"

I said, "I asked my cat if she knew who broke into our apartment and to show me who it was. She's telling on you! You broke into our apartment, didn't you?"

He was nervously defensive and said, "No! I didn't break into your house! You know I wouldn't do nuthin' like that!" Later we found out he actually did break in.

Worker Killed

It wasn't long after that break-in that we moved from our top floor apartment and kept our second floor apartment as our "spot." We moved into a very nice second floor apartment in a four-unit building with a very nice landlord where she and her daughters occupied the other units.

When we moved in, we started an extensive rehab project on it. We dropped ceilings, painted, and put in new carpeting throughout. We redid the kitchen and added doors to the living room, turning it into a master bedroom. We did everything to prepare our place for my daughters, my husband and I. We then furnished the place in luxury. For our master bedroom, I got a white marble topped black lacquer bedroom set with two large armoires and dresser with a vanity in the middle. Each of the two armoires had two drawers on the bottom. The white marble-topped nightstands were connected to the bed through the white marble topped mirrored headboard. It was the most beautiful bedroom I had ever seen. I have never seen one like it since.

I remember getting a beautiful canopy bedroom set for my youngest daughter and my other daughter got a beautiful white bedroom set. We were on our way—or so I thought.

Right after that, he got me a brand new beautiful black car. A week after we got the car, my husband asked me if he could borrow it to pick up a friend on the south side. On the way back, he ran it into a pole and totaled the car. We hadn't gotten insurance on it yet, so that was the end of that.

However, as trouble would have it, we experienced a catastrophic turn of events right there at our spot. One of the families on the first floor of our building had a relative that had been jailed for some time, and once he got out, he moved in with them. As it turns, out this relative was a former heroin dealer, and through observing the goings on in the building, had found out about our spot, and he figured we could do some dealings together and asked the drug dealer if he could join forces with us; he would offer heroin and we would continue with our preferred marijuana. My husband would not have it because heroin is such an addictive drug that it would have brought in a whole new group of people to the building. Heroin is not a recreational drug like marijuana. Heroin addicts absolutely HAVE to have it. These people would steal, stick people up, or do anything they had to in order to get their drug. Nobody in the apartment building would be safe. Instead, my husband offered him a job selling our choice drug. It was marijuana or nothing. My husband insisted. The young man agreed and became our new hire.

It was not unusual for thieves to want what we had, so one day some of them came in to stick us up. My husband's brother and our new worker were in the hallway. While they were waiting for customers, two men came into the hallway and asked for some marijuana. My brother-in-law went upstairs to get the marijuana, and when he came out of the apartment with it, standing at at the top of the stairs, he heard the men say "This is a stickup!" and he ran out the back door. The new hire started to run as well, but they shot him in the head and he died instantly. When I heard about it, I was devastated. I couldn't help but feel it was our fault. If we hadn't hired that man, he would still be alive. Years later I found out it had nothing to do with us, but instead it was related to something that happened when he was in jail.

I was relieved his mother didn't blame us at all. She didn't have any money, so she couldn't afford to pay for her son's funeral, so the drug dealer and I contributed to it and even attended. What disturbed me as much as the murder was the fact that I saw only about ten people in attendance. I would think at least some of his relatives would be there, but there was nobody (and I mean nobody) there. I don't think they ever found out who murdered that man.

Throughout our marriage, there were always crack users hanging around our building, even family members trying to get us to use crack. I know that they were trying to get us addicted to crack because, once addicted, we would be their suppliers. Up until now, we always refused their offers. But now, in our weakend state because of our guilt, it wasn't hard at all to convince us to use crack to drown our sorrow. So we started using crack. My drug dealer husband always said it was my fault for getting him addicted to crack, but that's not true. When anyone decides to take a hit, to smoke a joint, to smoke a cigarette to take a drink, it's always your choice to take that first hit. His addiction lasted years after I became clean. I guess that was my fault also.

    The effect this event had on me put me back on crack in no time. This was the worst ride of my life. Emotionally, I went straight to hell. So, there I was, a crack addict all over again. A monster I thought would never capture me again did so through one emotionally traumatic thing after the other. In my weakened state, I returned to what was familiar.

Jackie's Sad End

My final story on Jackie the cat is a sad one. One day my second husband and I took a trip to the grocery store and left my daughters and Jackie at home. My oldest daughter was there, cleaning up the place a bit. She opened the back door to empty the garbage and the neighbor's pit bull was standing there. Jackie was standing right behind her and had noticed the pit bull standing in the open door. Jackie took off and attacked the pit before it came in to attack my daughter. It was horrific. My daughter was horrified at the fight between the two animals. Someone had rushed to the supermarket to tell us what was going on, and I dropped everything and got home in time to see that Jackie had been mauled pretty badly. There was blood everywhere, so we rushed her to the vet.

She had been fatally wounded. The pit bull had torn out her vagina so the doctor informed us that she would need to be put to sleep. We grieved bitterly but she had saved my daughter's life. Thank you, God.

Going to Church

At this time, my husband and I struggled between addiction and God. We both peeked in the church more and more until we decided to join the King David Church where my brother used to be assistant pastor, but at this time, he had become pastor of his own church on the south side of Chicago. We even had our children baptized there. We wanted to be fully involved with the church, so we both joined the choir. We felt bad about the business we were in and tried as much as we could to distance ourselves from it (especially while at church), but since it was our livelihood, there was an obvious conflict. How can we be devout Christians and yet sell drugs for a living? We were sure God was not pleased about this. In any case, we were seen attending services and singing in the choir, wearing luxurious attire. We were admired for how well dressed we were, but unknown (or known) to other members, it was all bootlegged, stolen, or bought with drug money. Maybe since we were part of the world, we could say we didn't know better, or maybe we were in a state of denial. In fact, after many services, we would go and get high together. Looking back at it now, I can't believe we disrespected God like that, but because of God's faithful, generous, forgiving, everlasting, promising, and hopeful love, years later he delivered me from myself. Maybe if Paul, a former persecutor of Christians, can be forgiven so could we. What I learned is that we shouldn't wait until we are clean to attend or join a church. A lot of people may think, "Oh no! I can't go to church until I get my life together!" But we need to come as we are because we might not survive in the world in order to make it back to church; it's God who will give us the strength to resist the devil and make him flee.

Perfect Peace

In all, I have experienced ultimate peace that surpasses any understanding at least three times in my life and can say that I honestly know what it feels like to die. God showed me. This shows that God is even more powerful than drug addiction, because even through the fog of drug addiction, he reached me. For instance, the first time I felt total peace was during my stay on LaCrosse (in Chicago).

One day I was laying on the couch and an unusual feeling started to come over me; it started at my feet and flowed very slowly up my legs, to my hips, my torso, until it made its way up to my head. I didn't know what it could be. I thought, *Oh my God, I'm dying!* I hadn't ever felt such a thing, not even being high. I literally began to feel as if I had died, but it was inexplicably peaceful. No words have ever been created on this side of heaven that can possibly explain this absolute and total peace—the complete freedom from any earthly pain or concern—the ultimate joy. In this place, it was so peaceful that not even thoughts about things we experience these days like earthquakes, hurricanes, floods, or drought could even enter your mind. There was no sin, evil, sorrow, pain, violence, nor injustice that could reach you there. It was complete peace, tranquility, and safety. It was something that could only come from God. I thought, *If this is what it's like to die, I don't want to come back.*

A year later, it came again, only this time it didn't frighten me as much as it did the first time. But I was curious as to why it was there again. Was God trying to prepare me to die? Maybe it was due to the doubt I felt the first time, so I accepted it. Months later, this same blanket of peace approached me for the last time, but this time I was prepared for it. I wanted it. And before it would engulf me, I made up my mind that no one or nothing was going to stop me from enjoying it. I got up and went to the window and watched the kids playing outside as this sensation had its way with me; I wanted to embrace it right there in front of that window. No drug had ever made me feel this way. I asked God why I was feeling such a thing because I thought I was losing my mind, but John 14:27 says, "I leave you peace; my peace I give you. I do not give it to you as the world does. So don't let your hearts be troubled or afraid." From then on I searched all the days of my life to find someone else who had felt the same perfect peace I had felt, and it seemed nobody had. Some would say, "Oh yeah. I felt it." But I could tell by how nonchalantly they said it that they hadn't felt it. I finally found confirmation from another person when my family was working on funeral arrangements for my sister, Tina. Pastor Melvin and Assie Brown, pastor and first lady of my current church, King David MBC, were at my mother's house to comfort us as they had done previously at my two other brothers' funerals (which I will explain later). I happened to mention to them that my sister was in perfect peace now, and I knew the peace she must feel. I told them of my experience describing it as a peace beyond any understanding and Pastor Brown said, "I know exactly what you are talking about." And went on to describe his experience. He told me in words that I always longed to hear—how someone else felt the same things I have. Pastor Brown and his wife, Assie, have always been there for us. I knew then that they truly were men and women of God.

    I remember pastor Brown getting deathly ill. He had lost all his weight; he looked like he was standing on death's door. He was so sick he stopped ministering services and let his wife run the services. But just as he was slowly taken away from us, God slowly brought him back to us. When he returned to ministering the church, everyone could see how God was healing him before our very eyes. God demonstrated he is who he said he is as a healer. Look at God.

Two of the Drug Dealer's Friends Attack

It wasn't long after that when the drug dealer and I were separated. The struggle with the conflict between us being churchgoers and drug dealers continuously grew. It's like when the devil saw us trying to straighten our lives out, he had to increase his attack on us. Even after having a very meaningful church service, the holiness faded as soon as we got home. Before we even got into our door, there would be people hanging around asking to buy drugs and tempting us to get high with them. Eventually the world with its temptations won out (temporarily). More and more, my husband the drug dealer would stay over with his friends and associates, and I'd stay home and get high by myself.

Eventually I started seeing someone else, and one day my husband came over with one of his friends during our separation and saw me laying in bed with this new guy. He was furious and he and his friend walked out.

Soon after that, I was at home alone, getting high, and the doorbell rang. I looked out of the window and saw two men, one of which I recognized as one of the drug dealer's friends that live on the same block as his parents. He and my husband grew up together. They asked me, "Is your husband there?"

"No, he's not here," I said.

"Dag! I got some good stuff that I wanted to share with y'all! Hey, can we come up for a minute? You know us. We from Fulton!"

"Oh, okay," I said begrudgingly. "I'll come down and let you in." I thought to myself since the kids are out and nobody's here, it would be okay.

When I let them in, we went to the bar in the bedroom where we always got high, and they pulled out their stuff and we got high. They had several bags of cocaine on them, so we sat there for quite a while. After we finished, I walked them to the door. Before I could open the door, they grabbed me, dragged me back into my youngest girl's bedroom, threw me onto her bed, proceeded to tear off my clothes and began beating me, yelling, "If you scream I'll kill you! This is from your husband!" I was in total shock and terror and thought, *Oh my God! Are they going to kill me? Were they really sent by my husband? No! They couldn't be—not him—not from such a gentle, loving man who took me away from the street and took me to such wonderful places! The man who lovingly took care of my daughters. Not this churchgoing man who had such a beautiful singing voice in the choir!*

I was so humiliated, being in my baby's room with all of her innocent furnishings—all of her dolls lying there looking upward at the top of her bed's canopy. It's like not only was I defiled, but my daughter's room was defiled. What woke me up from this dream was a fist to my face. The attacks were so brutal I was sure I was going to die that night. When they stopped for a while, I heard the doorbell ring, and they looked at each other. I said, "Someone who knows I'm here is there. Can I please go to the window and tell them I'm busy so I can get rid of them?"

They looked at each other again and said, "Uh—okay—but you be right back here!" (The idiots!) So I painfully got up, wrapped myself in a sheet, and went to the window. On the way to the window, I unlocked the door in case someone could help me. I looked out and saw a tall, dark figure and I thought to myself, *Oh my God! It's Mr. C!* It was a friend of ours who was looking to come in and get high. I quickly raised the window and yelled out, crying to him, "Help me! I'm being raped and they're beating me!" He then frantically rang a bunch of the other doorbells in the outside of the apartment building so someone would let him in. When someone opened the building door, they asked him, "Did you hear the commotion?" Mr. C ran up the stairs to my apartment. At the same time, I raced to the apartment front door, being chased by the rapists. We all got to the door at the same time, but I managed to open the door and run out into the hall (because the door was unlocked—I had unlocked it when I had the chance to get to the door). The rapists were still standing inside the apartment.

When Mr. C saw me, he said to the two other men, "What happened to her? She says you raped and beat her!"

They said, "Man! We didn't do nothing to this woman! We was up here getting high! We don't know what's wrong with her."

He said, "Man you lying! Yes you did! Look at her! She's bleeding all over the place, her face is all swole up and where's her clothes? Man! Y'all raped her!"

"Man we didn't do nothin'!" the two men said, pushed Mr. C aside and ran down the hallway, disappearing into the night.

Mr. C said, "Go put some clothes on," and then asked, "What you want to do? Should we call the police?"

I said "No! Don't call the police! They said my husband sent them!" So Mr. C stayed with me the whole night to make sure I was safe. It quickly spread throughout the neighborhood what had happened. The next day, one of the people in the neighborhood came to me to see if what they heard was true and said, "I couldn't believe what I heard happened, but looking at you, I can see it's true. I couldn't believe it because I saw those same two men hanging out on Fulton, sitting on the front porch with your husband." I then immediately called my husband about it and he denied being involved at all. My husband not being involved? What do you think? I was physically and mentally messed up for weeks after that.

A few days later I went back to the basement where my husband now stayed, and my brother, the preacher, came over after hearing I was raped and how badly beaten I was, but I wouldn't come to the door because I couldn't stand to have him see me the way I was. The devil had me at that time. Can you see him (the devil)?

Drug Treatment

I knew then I needed help, and soon after decided to visit a drug treatment center. This was the first of many. While I was there, my parents were so relieved they gave me incentives like money for cigarettes and other things. But I saved the money and didn't buy cigarettes, candy, tampons, or anything. When I got out of rehab I went right back to my husband and got high with him, and that's what I used the money for.

One Center was Real Nice

The next time I went to a drug treatment center it was a real nice one. In this particular center there were just two women and about ten men. I had been there for several weeks, and so they decided they could let me out on a pass. As soon as I left, I used the money I had saved to buy drugs and came back to my room to share with my roommate. While we were getting high, the staff called everyone out to dinner and my roommate became so paranoid from the drugs that she locked herself into the bathroom and hid in the bathtub. I pleaded with her to come out. "Please come out! They're calling us for dinner! They'll know we been getting high!" In her paranoia, she screamed from behind the locked door that she couldn't because something was after her. I thought to myself, *Aw man, I'm in trouble*. The staff had to break down the door to get her out. The next day they asked us both to leave the center. I felt so bad about it because I not only risked my life but that of my roommate. We never spoke again.

Five-Dollar Man

Another thing that happened when I was in that rehab center was I met a guy who I thought was the cutest thing and we hit it off. We had a serious relationship during our time there. We made big plans about how we were going to get clean and get out of the center and how he was going to get a job. We were going to get married and have children. After I was kicked out of the rehab center, I was too humiliated and embarrassed to try to contact him so I considered that relationship as being "over." It was a few weeks after my humiliating exit, I just happened to be at my mother's house when the doorbell rang. It was him—my "boyfriend" from the rehab center, the man of my dreams, my prince charming. He was looking all clean and drug free—both mentally and physically. I was embarrassed and self conscious because I knew I did not look or feel clean or drug free. I just knew he could tell I was back on drugs. I didn't know until then that he had also left the center. I quickly and happily introduced him to my mother and invited him in. He told me how much he missed me and such. About the time he was ready to leave, we went outside and he pulled me aside, and to my surprise he said, "I got 5 dollars. If you get 5 dollars, we can get us a bag and we can get high." I thought to myself, *Oh my God! I guess he's not so clean after all! Maybe we can just get high this one time and then we can get us a job, a house, a new clean life and make all our dreams come true.* I borrowed 5 dollars and gave it to him. He said, "I'll just go up the street and get us a bag. You wait here. I'll be right back." I expectantly waited but he never came back, and I haven't seen him to this day. I guess he must have got lost! No boyfriend and no drugs!—and now I don't even have my 5 dollars! And that was the end of my five-dollar man.

40 oz

I remember another time when my husband was out getting high, leaving me alone, and so I went out and got high too. I met another man on the street that invited me back to his place to get high. Being as addicted as I was, I was perfectly agreeable to that. While at his place, he left to get more drugs, and I was just sitting around waiting for him to come back. So there I was, at 7:00 a.m, sitting in a large sunroom divided up into sections with sheets and doors. I could hear other people moving around. As I nervously glanced around the room, I noticed a number of 40-oz beer bottles laying around. They had their tops screwed down and looked full. I thought to myself, *I'm gonna have me one of those beers while I wait for him to come back with some more drugs.* When I unscrewed the top I thought it was funny it didn't snap like when you open the seal on a fresh bottle. I didn't give it another thought until I took a big swig and immediately spit it out in disgust. Oh my God! It was urine! Now, many drug addicts, when they have to pee, are often too lazy or too high to go to the bathroom to relieve themselves or don't want to leave their drugs unattended, so they pee in empty beer bottles and put the screw cap back on so they don't have to get up to throw them away. How far I have fallen and what depths God did redeem me from? (Got pee?) Just like the prodigal son in the Bible who had gotten so low that he would eat what was used to feed the pigs.

How My Parents Raised My Kids

My mother was really the guardian of my kids by then. In fact she kept them until they were out of high school. My youngest daughter quickly married (Rev. Anton presided) because she wanted stability. My oldest daughter moved out of the house. They were very involved in the church and remained so, even when I was no longer involved myself. They're still there. I felt like the one thing I did right was to introduce my children to the church and the way of the Lord before my life took such a drastic downturn. Just as the Bible says: "Train up a child in the way he should go: and when he is old, he will not depart from it" (KJV 22:6). This is a true example of this scripture.

The Stench of Sin

I remember when I started being so sick and tired of being sick and tired. I was walking up and down the street, in fact right across from where I lived. I remember mostly I started going to the back of my mother's house, sneaking off and getting high alone. I was getting so lonely—I remember feeling like God was taking his covering off me. I remember feeling like I was not alive anymore. Everything I had known about myself was gone. It was leaving. Everything: my personality, hygiene, my love for people, my kindness, my willingness to share.

One day, I was over at my mother's house, washing a pair of jeans I had on for over a week and then I hung them up and left them there to dry. Soon after that, my mother said she smelled this horrible odor and ran throughout the house looking for its source until she found my jeans hanging in the bathroom. My mother described it as smelling like a dirty, unwashed vagina that hadn't been cleaned for a month—it was terrible! I realize today that it was the stench of sin and it took me a long time to understand that it's a stench you can't wash away—only the blood of Jesus can wash the stench of sin away. Thank you Jesus for your grace and mercy to wash away my sin with your blood. Everything was leaving, diminishing. Things began looking dark and grim. Even if the sun was out, to me it was still dark. I started becoming jittery and fearful.

My Gruesome Time in the Alleys

Many nights as a drug addict, I walked the streets and alleys, sniffing about like a dog for drugs. Life was fitted for the streets at that time and getting high is what got me there. I'd always be looking for drugs, money, any kind of bag—and I found bags of cocaine many times. When I got high or even prepared to, my bowels would move; if I got money from my parents, 10 dollars from dad or mom, that would set it off. I knew what I'd buy with it and just at the anticipation of getting my drugs, my stomach would churn and I'd have to go. I guess it was a sign that I was about to get high, I don't know. When I had to go to the bathroom, I went right there. I'd go anywhere (I remember once I was in an alley). I'd stop, drop my pants and have a bowel movement—sometimes loose! When I was done, I'd pick up leaves, clean myself, and move on and resume my search. That was another one of my low points.

I Knew I Was Dying

I knew I was dying spiritually and physically. I could still hear the voice of the Lord telling me to call on him. One day I sat on my mother's back stoop and I just started crying and saying, "God I can't get off of this. The demons just won't leave me alone. It won't stop talking to me. I can't get away from these people, God! I can't get off this! I can't deal with my kids. I don't know them anymore. I can't do it!" I asked him to help me. If I had a dime in my pocket, my mind would start working, thinking, *All I need is another four dollars and ninety cents and I can get a nickel bag and get high.* At the time I was on welfare, and every month I would get my welfare check, which included food stamps and some cash. I would give my mom some of the food stamps and my kids a very little bit of the money. The rest of the money I would use to get high—and when I got high, I wouldn't eat, I wouldn't sleep, I wouldn't bathe, and I wouldn't want to be bothered with anyone. The only reason I got high with other addicts was because I needed others around so I wouldn't be alone with my drug induced paranoia. I was a sociable drug addict, but I didn't want too many people around because the money would go too fast. I didn't even want to leave the table to use the bathroom because I was afraid someone else at that table would take any drugs I had there away from me or even smoke the residue in my pipe. I wanted it all for me. I've seen a fellow female addict who would use sanitary napkins like a diaper so she wouldn't have to leave to use the bathroom.

My only worry was what I was going to do to get my next hit when the drugs were gone. The number one thought in a drug addict's head is "My next hit—where am I going to get the next hit?" Any time I got any money at all, my stomach would start boiling—my body was anticipating getting high. I began to realize I couldn't do it on my own. But eventually, gradually, God began taking the taste out of my mouth, but oh, how I struggled with relapses. I didn't realize at the time that the only way out was through Jesus Christ.

My Father's Dream

I remember the day my father told me about a dream he'd had about me. My father said, "Come here, girl," calling me into his bedroom. "Close the door." He said, "Last night I had a dream. I was on a boat. It was the most beautiful boat I ever saw. The weather was perfect, the sun was bright, and everyone on it was excited and happy that we were going on a wonderful trip. I'm not sure where to. It didn't seem to matter. Everything on the boat was perfect. It was like nothing I'd ever seen before. But then the bell rang that the boat was leaving, and I noticed everyone in the family was on board except you. I said, 'Wait a minute! Don't leave yet! Don't leave yet! My daughter is not on the boat!' And the man said, 'She better hurry up and get onboard, because she's going to miss the boat!' And I hollered to you, 'Come on! Come on! Get on the boat, girl! Run! Run! They're going to leave! And I saw you running, but the more you ran, the farther away you were. 'Come on, girl! Run!' And you screamed, 'Daddy! Don't let them leave me! Don't let them leave me, Daddy!' Then the boat finally pulled off and I hollered, 'You left my daughter behind! Please go back and get her!' And the man said, 'I'm sorry. We didn't leave without her, she missed the boat.' And you were hollering, 'Come back! Come back! Please don't let them leave me! Daddy! Don't let them leave me!'"

When I came to the house the sun was out and I was there and my intent was to ask for money so I could get drugs. After hearing that story from my father, I walked out of that house. It was dark out—the darkest I ever saw it. This was the first time I received what my father was saying. He was begging me to get off of those drugs. And God was telling both him and me that if I didn't get off those drugs, I would miss the boat which was on its way to heaven. I remembered all of the times my father would try to talk to me about quitting drugs. I would always get so mad at him for going to the drug rehab outreach meetings to get help at how he could help me get off of drugs. I never appreciated how much he was trying to do for me. That day I finally received every word he said and what God was saying through him. This was the beginning of the end to my addiction. SEE GOD?

Turning Point

That was a turning point for me; that was huge to me. I had really gotten tired. I had started meeting so many people, so many men in the neighborhood who just wanted me to get high with them. They didn't want anything concrete. They just wanted to pleasure themselves by looking at my body or even tasting it or some other such nonsense. To me it was disgusting because women that were on drugs were described as nasty. They were unclean inside and out, naturally and spiritually. I remember I just started feeling like I was going to die soon. In fact I knew I'd be dead soon. Death was coming for me; I was surrounded by it. Everyone else I knew was dying and I was next. But I could hear a voice saying, *Just call on me. Just call on me.* Then I would hear another voice saying, *You better go get another hit. It's too late for you; you're gonna die. You have gone too far, nobody loves you anymore, you're out here all by yourself now. You have disappointed your family, your kids are all split up. It's too late for you.*

Lamont

I remember one day, I was at my mother's house and my brother Lamont showed up. We were both visiting for a while and I finally decided to leave to go down the street and get high with my husband. When I got to the door to leave, Lamont decided to leave too, and as we both stepped outside, he said, "I need someone to talk to." I said "Okay," slightly puzzled because I thought, *Why would he want to talk to me? He knows I'm probably going to hit him up for some money.*

As we walked to the corner in the direction I was headed, he sighed, saying, "I'm so tired—so tired of having so many people over at my house all the time. Just all that drinking, partying, and playing cards and getting high. I'm just tired of it." His girlfriend had many friends and family that were constantly coming over, partying, and staying for days, and even weeks.

I said, "Maybe you should move back in with your wife and son?"

He said, "I don't think they'd take me back, and I don't blame them for not taking me back." He then gave me some money, gave me a hug, and walked towards his car. I don't know why, but I couldn't help feeling sorry for him, and as I walked to where I was going, I kept watching him as he walked to his car, got in, and drove away. I didn't realize it then, but that was the last time I saw my brother walking on his own.

Lamont's Stroke

The next day my brother Lamont tried to get out of bed as usual to go to the bathroom, but instead he fell to the floor. His girlfriend who he was living with at the time, said, "Hey, Lamont. What are you doing on the floor? Get up."

He said, "I can't." She kept yelling, "Get up! Get up off that floor!" He later told me he cried for help several times "Help me! Help me!" and it was as if she didn't even care or want to help him. He said he had to cry for help for a long time before his girlfriend believed there was actually a serious problem and finally called the ambulance.

On that day my parents received a phone call: They were told he was in the hospital and that he had a stroke.

A couple of days later, when my family and I were visiting him at the hospital, we saw him walking up and down the hallway with a big smile on his face, being helped by his son, Scotty, and with a cane. We were overjoyed at that sight; we were sure he was going to be all right. But a couple of days later things turned for the worse. He couldn't get up anymore, and the left side of his face was drooping and twisted from the stroke.

About couple of weeks later, we went to the hospital and he surprised us by telling us he was going to marry his girlfriend. He told us she had suggested that since his benefits were going to end from work, he could then be covered by hers from the same company where they both worked. I thought to myself, *That's a load of crap! I knew she didn't care about his coverage from benefits. She thinks he's going to die and then she would get all of his possessions, including any bank accounts or money he had.*

Everyone, including me and my father, asked him, "Are you sure this is what you want?" We knew Lamont was not in his right mind because of the stroke, and he was heavily medicated. But that is what he decided to do.

Lamont and his girlfriend were married right in the hospital. On the same day, as soon as the wedding was over, his new wife made some excuse that she had to leave and promptly disappeared.

About a month after that—surprise! He was released from the hospital and sent home even though he needed constant care. His stroke left him totally debilitated: he needed to be fed, clothed, bathed, helped using the toilet, and his wife had to be his caregiver. This was something I'm sure his new wife didn't expect or enjoy in the least.

After about a month, my mom got a knock on her door. It was Lamont and his new wife. She said she could no longer care for him and dropped him off, leaving him there, never to retrieve him. From then on, my parents were his constant caregivers. They fed him, they bathed him and took him to the doctor, as well as made sure he took his medication. My parents were not young anymore, but they insisted on caring for him. "He is our son and the only acceptable thing to do is care for him."

Move to Wisconsin

The west side of Chicago had proven to be too much for me and I needed a change, ready or not. However, I was scared and I didn't want to leave my husband. Nonetheless, God obviously heard my desire because that's when my sister and her husband came to get me. I was in the basement of the building where my husband now lived and I was about to get high when I heard a loud knock on the door. Then I heard a loud voice telling me, "Come on! It's time to go!"

I thought to myself, *That sounds like my brother-in-law.*

"Go where?" I said.

"To Milwaukee! Your sister's out in the car waiting for you. We came to get you! You're going with us!" he said.

I said, "I ain't going nowhere!"

"Yes, you are! Now come on! You're going with us!" With that, he picked me up, threw me over his shoulder, and bodily carried me out the door.

"No! Let me go! I ain't going nowhere!" I screamed to my husband, "Make him put me down! If I do go, are you going with me?"

My brother-in-law said to my drug dealer husband, "You wanna go too?"

"Naw. I got things to do," he said. "Go on and take her, man. Maybe I can get myself together. If it wasn't for her, I wouldn't be on drugs anyway." My brother-in-law threw me in the car, got in, and pulled off with me kicking and screaming in the back seat.

His wife, my sister, was in full agreement and smiled with tears in her eyes. I went kicking and screaming—literally. "I can't leave my husband yet! I can't leave my husband!" But I realize today that I wasn't afraid of leaving my husband, I was afraid of leaving my drugs. He was the representation of my dependency on drugs. I cried and carried on for a while during the ride, but they were very gentle with me. They fed me and tried to talk sense into my head. Once I got there, that's when God had a chance to really minister and talk to me. Their home was beautiful and orderly. I could breathe there. I could hear God clearly. I kept drinking but didn't get high on cocaine anymore. Improvement, I guess. My sister took me in just as I was and did an excellent job of cleaning me up and paying for a new look for me by way of loving shopping sprees, etc.

Unfortunately, I could find no real resolve at my sister's house because my brother-in-law started watching me closely. He was convinced that I was a thieving crackhead who would steal everything in sight as soon as I was left alone in their house—and who could blame him?

One day, I decided to surprise them before they got home from work by cleaning their house and cooking one of my seven-course home-cooked meals. I'd prepared it just for the two of them to enjoy at the end of their workday. When they came home and tried to get in, they'd found that I had put the double lock on the door, and my brother-in-law started banging on the door, yelling, "Open the door! Let us in! She's ripping us off!" As I was setting the table, I yelled, "Just a minute! Just a minute! I'll let you in!" When they came in, he immediately ran upstairs to the bedroom to see if I had stolen anything, but my sister stopped in the kitchen door. She saw the table spread with all the dishes I had prepared and smelled all the wonderful food I'd cooked just for them. From upstairs my brother-in-law yelled, "My jewelry is missing!" He then came down and, looking at me, said, "I can't find my jewelry. She ripped us off!"

My sister was very surprised and turned and stared at her husband with dismay. My sister always believed in me. She said, "Don't say that! You probably misplaced it! You'll find it. She was in the kitchen cooking dinner for us."

Looking at me, he said, "You can fool her but you can't fool me."

After a couple of days, he found the missing jewelry and she told him to apologize—which he did—begrudgingly—

but by then I had decided it was time for me to go. But where? Not to Chicago. By this time my drug dealer husband had started dating somebody else.

Second Husband's Girlfriend

I remember my second husband's girlfriend, Lily. Oh, how she wanted to be like me. She even wanted to be called Lil, as I was affectionately called by those who knew me. I had left my drug dealer husband and gotten clean, so she'd be my replacement I guess; there was still a Lil to call his own. She tried to dress like me as much as her fashion prowess would allow her to; in too many ways she tried to rebuild herself to be my mimic. By then I had stopped doing drugs. Perhaps that's what she secretly admired the most, especially since she was still strung out on the pipe and remained so until she died of a heart attack in that very basement while smoking a crack pipe. I think to myself, *That could have been me if I had stayed in Chicago with him,* and I thank the Lord for delivering me from that environment.

She (My Sister) Always Said Good Things About Me

My sister Tina always said good things about me and gave me endless encouragement. She declared to me that I would write a book one day. I told her I always wanted to do real estate, and she always told me I'd be successful. Everything she said was always life-giving to me. Even after I moved out of her house, my sister always believed in me, and it kept me going. Her voice was among those of my mother, father, and siblings encouraging me to do my best. They believed that I would defeat crack addiction and become something of worth, but I had to believe it myself.

Living in Milwaukee—A Rehab Experience Like None Other

Living in Milwaukee was a rehab experience like none other. Well, after a while, my brother-in-law, who worked as a news writer at one of the local colleges, had introduced me to one of his friends. I had moved out of my sister's house and moved in for a short time with this guy I had met. Well, he wasn't just a guy; he was a college professor at the local college I started attending. By now I had gotten a job as a waitress at Red Lobster and I was still drinking. I liked my job there and did well there. I'd made a couple of friends, one of which was the hostess. She was easy to laugh and talk with, which perhaps I did a little too much—talking, that is. I'd told her my story of drug use and my present day effort to resist, and that is when she informed me that her boyfriend sold drugs and she thought that we should connect. "Really?" I said. "Well, I'm not in recovery yet. I'm trying to dry out on my own," I tried to tell her. "So, meeting your boyfriend is not the thing to do right now." But we did anyhow and I bought drugs from him and sneaked it back to where I was living at the time. To add insult to injury, she and I not only worked together, but she and her boyfriend lived across the street from me. They became my drug hawks. Every time my boyfriend went to work and I was home alone, they made sure I got drugs, pipes, and anything else I needed to enhance my high. I had stashed my new paraphernalia in my boyfriend's house, and when he'd go to work I would get my pipe from where I'd hidden it on top of the fridge and pack it real good, light it up, and get high. This new venture with new suppliers lasted all of a week.

For some reason this time it was not something I felt I could continue to do. *I can't do this anymore,* I said to myself. After confessing to my boyfriend that I'd been getting high in his house, I voluntarily walked myself through the doors of another drug treatment center; this time I wanted help. At forty-two years old, I had to make this my last relapse.

HIV Test

As soon as I arrived at the center, I was tested for any diseases I may currently have, as was the standard for new patients, and went immediately to participate in group sessions. However, a little more than a week later, I was sitting in one of the sessions when a nurse came and whispered that they needed to speak to me. They pulled me out of the session and escorted me to an office where a nurse and a couple of counselors sat waiting for my arrival. I didn't know what to expect and I was a little nervous. I thought, *What could they want to talk to me about?* They said they had my results from the tests I had taken when I entered the center. They told me I had tested positive for HIV. Hearing the word *positive* almost killed me on the spot. I cried hysterically.

I was allowed to call my family; I called my mother first and told her that I was HIV positive. We both sobbed on the phone for a long time. My heart was broken irretrievably. "Mom, tell the family," I whimpered. From there I called the guy I was living with and broke the news and his response was, "Don't cry. When you get out, I'm going to buy you a new car." *Huh?* I thought. *What am I gonna do with a new car? I'm gonna die!* Nothing mattered because now I was dying (and maybe he was too)!

The counselors saw that I was depressed beyond repair and told me I didn't have to participate in group sessions if I didn't want to. "Would you just like to stay in your room?" they asked.

"Yes, please," I responded. I stayed in that room for several days, praying and admitting to God that I had sinned, asking for his forgiveness and promising him if he would save me, I would serve him until I die. With all the things I had done in my life, I could not believe God would forgive me because I was a sinner on my way to hell.

The treatment center visit and the treatment within was supposed to be thirty days long, but given my circumstances they let me out after only two weeks. Upon my exit, I was tested again for HIV/AIDS. Going home to wait for the results was torture; those days seemed like years, but lo and behold, two days later my phone rang, and this time I knew they had the results on how bad it was—how long I had to live. I knew I was dead. When I answered the phone, the nurse said, "I'm so sorry. I am SO SORRY." I just started crying and waited to hear her tell me the time I had left on earth. But instead she said, "We have NEVER made a mistake like this. You don't have AIDS." My promise to serve God was real. I fully believe that the test results were correct, but God spared me because of my vow to Him and that was to serve him until the day I die. Do you see him now?

When my friend the hostess at Red Lobster hooked me up with her boyfriend as a drug source, her and her boyfriend in their minds were just trying to get my money but, not realizing it, they actually saved my life. If they hadn't started me on drugs again, I never would have entered that drug treatment center and would never have found I had AIDS—and then would never have given myself to God. If that didn't happen, I would have fallen back into addiction and eventually died of AIDS.

The most important moment of my entire life was when I asked God for forgiveness, gave him my life, and promised I would serve him until I die. Can you stop and take a moment with me now to give God praise? DO YOU SEE HIM NOW?

The Baby

After I had moved in with the college professor, not long after my HIV experience, my youngest daughter and her husband came to Milwaukee and moved in with us. She was pregnant. Towards the end of her pregnancy, we went to South Carolina to visit his family. While we were there, she had a beautiful baby boy. His name was Savon Beal. When we returned from South Carolina, the baby was a few days old. I was so excited about my youngest daughter's first child! My grandson! My daughter was so proud, and I was also proud of them both! I was so proud of him because I knew I would be able to be a good grandma. All I could think of was shopping for him, what I was going to do for him, what schools he was going to go to—Grandma was ready to take over!

I was still working at Red Lobster, and I was on my way to work one morning and the spirit told me, "Sit down!" and I sat on the couch. I thought to myself, *Why am I sitting here? I'll be late for work!* I then heard a scream from the other room. It was my youngest daughter, crying and running out, holding her baby, who was motionless and had blood dripping from his nose. She passed him to me and I nervously passed him back to her. I didn't know what was going on. Finally she passed him to me again and said, "Momma! Take my baby! He's not breathing!" We rushed him to the hospital, where he was revived. But, sadly, after a couple of hours, he died. We found out that when he was born, he had an infection. We were both devastated. We brought the baby back to Chicago where he was buried. After the death of her baby, my daughter and her husband could not stand to live in that house in Milwaukee, so they moved back to Chicago.

A few months later, after the baby died, things became strained between the professor and I. I knew then I really needed God, so I then joined Jeremiah Missionary Baptist Church, which was led by the late Rev. Fred Boyd. It was right around the corner from his house. After a few months as a member there, I joined the choir (The Voices of Jeremiah) and became a faithful Sunday school student.

I remember one day while sitting in Sunday school class, the teacher came up to me and asked me if I wanted to teach the teenage class. I told her, "I don't know enough about God to teach a Sunday school class." But she said the spirit had told her that I was supposed to teach that class and besides they were short staffed, so I obeyed, and for the next five years I taught Sunday school and then became the assistant to the Sunday school secretary. After a while, they trusted me so much that after Sunday offering, they would let me count the money. Life was becoming good to me.

The professor didn't like the church. He wanted to keep drinking and partying and resented the fact I gave my life back to God. I eventually moved out. It was just me and God now. Finally, God had me to himself.

The Taste of Cigarettes

After moving out of the professor's house, I moved into my own apartment. I didn't have car or anything, but my parents were so proud of me that they helped me get a new car. I didn't last in that apartment too long because I met a woman whose name was Jessie—a faithful, awesome woman of God. She was a bit older than I was, and she joined the choir on the same day I did. We became best friends. It just so happens that as soon as we met, an apartment upstairs from her became vacant. I didn't want to be alone, so I moved from my apartment into the new one upstairs from Jessie.

I was still a cigarette smoker at the time and had been praying for God to take the taste of cigarettes from my mouth. When I moved into my apartment, I had caught a cold and didn't smoke because I wasn't feeling well (so I thought). A couple of days later I still didn't feel well and didn't smoke. After a week, I felt better and noticed I still hadn't smoked and had no desire to smoke and was amazed. God had removed the taste of cigarettes from my mouth and I didn't even know it! I haven't had a cigarette since! I was a cigarette smoker for twenty-seven years and just like that, the taste was taken out of my mouth, and now the stench of cigarettes is unbearable to me. I had been delivered. Can you see my almighty God?

Visiting Lamont

Now that I was living in Milwaukee, I still made it a point to visit my brother Lamont at my parents' house. I remember one time when I was visiting, I came into the living room; I saw Lamont sitting in his usual spot, and he would always break out into a big smile as soon as he saw me, like he was just waiting for me to come and was so happy to see me. During each visit, he always asked if I would pray with him, and we would pray together for healing and mercy.

During one of my visits, he was gleefully talking up a storm about every subject that came to him while we were all watching TV. My mother said, "Be quiet, we're trying to watch TV." His smile left and was replaced by a look of despair. I still remember him sadly saying, "I just wanted to have some adult company and conversation."

Anton's (Mickey's) Stroke

My oldest daughter took her time and ended up marrying eventually. Two months after my brother Rev. Anton Davis performed the marriage of my oldest daughter to her new husband, I got a phone call. It was my brother's wife Julie and she said that he was just rushed to the hospital by ambulance. She told me she had been reading the night before, fell asleep on the couch and early the next morning, she heard him cry out to her, "Julie! Help me!" She ran into the room and found him laying on the floor at the side of the bed unable to move. After some time, she was finally able to convince him that she should call an ambulance. He didn't want an ambulance called because he felt that if we just gave it a few minutes, he'd recover himself and be able to get up. He made her promise not to tell his mother because he thought everything was going to be all right. Later I found out through reports from the ambulance driver he began to become incoherent on the way to the hospital—he said things that didn't make sense. By the time he got there, word had got out and my mother, father, and myself arrived at the hospital. His wife did the right thing: she informed us what happened. Then some of her family members showed up too.

At the hospital, they had us all sit in a small waiting room because the doctor wanted to speak to the whole family. I can still remember it like it was yesterday. I remember where I was sitting and my parents were sitting right next to me. Julie and her family were sitting across from us. I can even remember what she wore. I can remember the gym shoes she wore because when the doctor came in, he informed us that Rev. Anton Davis (better known as Mickey) was brain dead. Immediately, Julie stood up and passed out. All I could see was the bottom of her gym shoes.

When we heard what the doctor said, my parents immediately turned towards me as if they wanted me to do something. I could only look back at them in disbelief. We didn't cry; nobody said anything because we were all in such shock. The next thing I remember after that was we were kneeling by his bed, praying. I remember the silent ride home in my parents' car, and as I looked out the window, I could see people walking up and down the street, talking with each other, laughing, children playing. They were carrying on their normal lives as if nothing was wrong. I thought to myself, *How can these people be happy? How can they act as if nothing happened? Don't they know Mickey's dead?*

I remember later that night I went back to the hospital when people who knew him were gathered in the waiting room. My family, brothers, sisters and Julie's family were all there, as well as some of his church members. Some of my cousins were preparing to go into Mickey's room to see him, pray over him, and say their goodbyes. One of the church members said to Julie, "Do you want me to keep these people out of his room?" I don't remember Julie answering him one way or the other because she was in shock but after hearing what he said, I went ballistic. "These people? What do you mean by 'these people'? These people are his family—brothers, sisters, and cousins who grew up with him. We knew him before any of you church people ever met him!"

My family said, "That's okay—we don't have to go in there." I felt my family should be able to go to his room, but they decided not to go—I went anyway. I then talked to my brother and spent time with him in his unconscious state. As I sat there in his room, looking at him, I thought, *God, why did you take him? He was a minister—a man of God—doing your work. Why is he lying there in that bed instead of me? Why didn't you take me? I'm the drug addict. I'm the partier, living the wild life—not him.*

It seemed he could have done so much more for the world than me. What a waste. I wondered why God skipped me.

On the way out of his room, walking toward the elevator, I heard a man loudly crying and carrying on. I saw it was a member of Mickey's church. It was the same man that had asked Julie if she wanted him to keep her family members out of Mickey's room. By then, I'd had it with everyone and I was struck with a feeling of burning rage. *How dare he cry like he cared for Mickey as much as I did! He didn't know and love Mickey like I did! He didn't grow up with him! Mickey was my brother!* I walked up to him and fiercely screamed, "Shut up! You just shut up!" And he did. I know that what I did wasn't the right thing to do, but I was in shock and everything really bothered me to the point where the slightest thing sent me into an uncontrollable rage.

Mickey's Funeral

The next thing I remember, I was sitting around the kitchen table at his house working on funeral arrangements for Mickey with his wife. After his death, he left behind his wife, Julie and his three children: daughters Jana and Jalisa, and son Jeremiah. I stayed close with Julie from then and onward after the funeral; we needed each other to get through this difficult time.

I remember going to the funeral home to view the remains of my brother in the casket. The funeral was huge. It was an awesome home-going. One thing that stuck out in my mind was sitting there watching people viewing the remains before the ceremony. I saw my brother's oldest daughter Jana, sitting there with a totally lost look of disbelief, as if to say, "Where am I?"

I also remember my brother Lamont sitting there. He looked so sad, sitting in that wheelchair, looking at Mickey in his casket. I was sure Lamont was wishing he could get up out of that chair and help in some way, but he couldn't. I was sure he was thinking, *Why did he die instead of me? He was the good one. The man of God. A pastor. I was the drinker, the partier. I was the one who left my wife and son for another woman. I should have been the one who died—not him.* I realize now that the reason my brother Mickey died right away when he had his stroke was that God knew he was ready to go home, and Lamont wasn't spiritually ready to be accepted onto heaven—and I myself wasn't. But Lamont did find God when he and I prayed together all those times I visited him. He began to grow spiritually.

I remember bringing a small Bible that my mother gave me to Mickey's funeral. She gave me that Bible, which was given to her by Lamont's wife, Teen (the only woman I acknowledge as Lamont's wife). She gave it to me because her eyes were getting older and could no longer read the small printing in that little Bible.

About three weeks after my brother Mickey's funeral, I couldn't find that little Bible anywhere. I called Julie and asked her to look around his church and their home for my Bible and they couldn't find it. I called everyone to look for it. For three weeks I looked everywhere and couldn't find it. One day I was lying in my bed, talking on the phone with Julie, and I happened to look on my nightstand and saw it. The Bible I was looking for all this time was suddenly there, and it was bookmarked at Revelations chapters 21 and 22, which described how beautiful heaven was. What an awesome revelation! I knew my brother was telling me he was ok. Here is what it said (from the King James version):

> *Revelations 21 And I saw a new heaven and a new earth: for the first heaven and the first earth were passed away; and there was no more sea.*
>
> *[2] And I John saw the holy city, new Jerusalem, coming down from God out of heaven, prepared as a bride adorned for her husband.*
>
> *[3] And I heard a great voice out of heaven saying, Behold, the tabernacle of God is with men, and he will dwell with them, and they shall be his people, and God himself shall be with them, and be their God.*
>
> *[4] And God shall wipe away all tears from their eyes; and there shall be no more death, neither sorrow, nor crying, neither shall there be any more pain: for the former things are passed away.*
>
> *[5] And he that sat upon the throne said, Behold, I make all things new. And he said unto me, Write: for these words are true and faithful.*

⁶ And he said unto me, It is done. I am Alpha and Omega, the beginning and the end. I will give unto him that is athirst of the fountain of the water of life freely.

⁷ He that overcometh shall inherit all things; and I will be his God, and he shall be my son.

⁸ But the fearful, and unbelieving, and the abominable, and murderers, and whoremongers, and sorcerers, and idolaters, and all liars, shall have their part in the lake which burneth with fire and brimstone: which is the second death.

⁹ And there came unto me one of the seven angels which had the seven vials full of the seven last plagues, and talked with me, saying, Come hither, I will shew thee the bride, the Lamb's wife.

¹⁰ And he carried me away in the spirit to a great and high mountain, and shewed me that great city, the holy Jerusalem, descending out of heaven from God,

¹¹ Having the glory of God: and her light was like unto a stone most precious, even like a jasper stone, clear as crystal;

¹² And had a wall great and high, and had twelve gates, and at the gates twelve angels, and names written thereon, which are the names of the twelve tribes of the children of Israel:

¹³ On the east three gates; on the north three gates; on the south three gates; and on the west three gates.

¹⁴ And the wall of the city had twelve foundations, and in them the names of the twelve apostles of the Lamb.

¹⁵ And he that talked with me had a golden reed to measure the city, and the gates thereof, and the wall thereof.

¹⁶ And the city lieth foursquare, and the length is as large as the breadth: and he measured the city with the reed, twelve thousand furlongs. The length and the breadth and the height of it are equal.

¹⁷ And he measured the wall thereof, an hundred and forty and four cubits, according to the measure of a man, that is, of the angel.

¹⁸ And the building of the wall of it was of jasper: and the city was pure gold, like unto clear glass.

¹⁹ And the foundations of the wall of the city were garnished with all manner of precious stones. The first foundation was jasper; the second, sapphire; the third, a chalcedony; the fourth, an emerald;

²⁰ The fifth, sardonyx; the sixth, sardius; the seventh, chrysolyte; the eighth, beryl; the ninth, a topaz; the tenth, a chrysoprasus; the eleventh, a jacinth; the twelfth, an amethyst.

²¹ And the twelve gates were twelve pearls: every several gate was of one pearl: and the street of the city was pure gold, as it were transparent glass.

²² And I saw no temple therein: for the Lord God Almighty and the Lamb are the temple of it.

^{23} And the city had no need of the sun, neither of the moon, to shine in it: for the glory of God did lighten it, and the Lamb is the light thereof.

^{24} And the nations of them which are saved shall walk in the light of it: and the kings of the earth do bring their glory and honour into it.

^{25} And the gates of it shall not be shut at all by day: for there shall be no night there.

^{26} And they shall bring the glory and honour of the nations into it.

^{27} And there shall in no wise enter into it any thing that defileth, neither whatsoever worketh abomination, or maketh a lie: but they which are written in the Lamb's book of life.

Revelations 22 And he shewed me a pure river of water of life, clear as crystal, proceeding out of the throne of God and of the Lamb.

^{2} In the midst of the street of it, and on either side of the river, was there the tree of life, which bare twelve manner of fruits, and yielded her fruit every month: and the leaves of the tree were for the healing of the nations.

^{3} And there shall be no more curse: but the throne of God and of the Lamb shall be in it; and his servants shall serve him:

^{4} And they shall see his face; and his name shall be in their foreheads.

^{5} And there shall be no night there; and they need no candle, neither light of the sun; for the Lord God giveth them light: and they shall reign for ever and ever.

⁶ And he said unto me, These sayings are faithful and true: and the Lord God of the holy prophets sent his angel to shew unto his servants the things which must shortly be done.

⁷ Behold, I come quickly: blessed is he that keepeth the sayings of the prophecy of this book.

⁸ And I John saw these things, and heard them. And when I had heard and seen, I fell down to worship before the feet of the angel which shewed me these things.

⁹ Then saith he unto me, See thou do it not: for I am thy fellowservant, and of thy brethren the prophets, and of them which keep the sayings of this book: worship God.

¹⁰ And he saith unto me, Seal not the sayings of the prophecy of this book: for the time is at hand.

¹¹ He that is unjust, let him be unjust still: and he which is filthy, let him be filthy still: and he that is righteous, let him be righteous still: and he that is holy, let him be holy still.

¹² And, behold, I come quickly; and my reward is with me, to give every man according as his work shall be.

¹³ I am Alpha and Omega, the beginning and the end, the first and the last.

¹⁴ Blessed are they that do his commandments, that they may have right to the tree of life, and may enter in through the gates into the city.

¹⁵ For without are dogs, and sorcerers, and whoremongers, and murderers, and idolaters, and whosoever loveth and maketh a lie.

¹⁶ I Jesus have sent mine angel to testify unto you these things in the churches. I am the root and the offspring of David, and the bright and morning star.

¹⁷ And the Spirit and the bride say, Come. And let him that heareth say, Come. And let him that is athirst come. And whosoever will, let him take the water of life freely.

¹⁸ For I testify unto every man that heareth the words of the prophecy of this book, If any man shall add unto these things, God shall add unto him the plagues that are written in this book:

¹⁹ And if any man shall take away from the words of the book of this prophecy, God shall take away his part out of the book of life, and out of the holy city, and from the things which are written in this book.

²⁰ He which testifieth these things saith, Surely I come quickly. Amen. Even so, come, Lord Jesus.

²¹ The grace of our Lord Jesus Christ be with you all. Amen.

Insurance Agent

Following my return home to get my life together after burying my baby brother, I returned to my job at Red Lobster. During one of my shifts, I was waiting on a table with a large group of well-dressed, well-spoken black women, and I asked them, "What y'all do for a living?"

They said, "We're insurance agents." And they pointed to the most well-dressed woman at the table, who seemed to be holding a meeting with everyone, and said, "That's Cynthia. She's our manager at the insurance company."

Cynthia was a beautiful, well-educated, well-spoken black woman. Before I knew it, I said "I want to be an insurance agent!" and she gave me her card and told me if I was serious to give her a call. So weeks later, I gave her a call and she explained to me that I would need to go to school and get licensed to become an insurance sales person. I said I would. She told me first I'd have to come in for an interview, and I did. After being interviewed, she told me she had enough staff under her, but she recommended I be interviewed by one of her comanagers. She said she'd go get him, and when she returned, in walked this tall, extremely well-educated, handsome dark-skinned black man named Leslie. Leslie was the kind of man who I could tell was extremely serious about his business and he seemed mean to me. I thought he would never hire me, but after talking with him (and I thought he'd never stop talking), he said, "If you take those classes and pass those license tests and get your license, I'll hire you." And that's exactly what I did. Not only did I tell Leslie he was going to hire me, but I told him I would be the best sales agent he'd ever had (which would take a miracle only God could perform, because I knew no-one in Milwaukee)! After passing my licensing tests and getting my license, I worked very hard to do as I promised—to become his number one agent.

Every month at my insurance company, they would list top agents and their figures on a board that everyone could see. They rated the agents in order of their sales figures. While I worked there, I made the board several times: I was always either number two or even number one.

At the peak of my insurance career, I had a car accident and was laid up for over a month. By then, the policies I were keeping track of started lapsing, so I decided I needed to do something else. I thought to myself, *If I can be this much of a success selling insurance, I can do anything!* I started thinking I wanted to be a real estate agent. While I was thinking about this, I just happened to be talking to a lender named Debbie Currie and we seemed to hit it off, so she had me talk to her boss, and he hired me on the spot as a lender. She and I became great friends as she taught me about lending. I had worked there for a month, during which time I was working with eight buyers to get them preapproved for loans. While working with them on their preapprovals, I thought to myself, *Why not follow my real passion and become a real estate agent so I can sell these people houses myself?* So that's what I did: while working with people on loans I took real estate classes, I got my real estate license and became a real estate agent. It just so happens that when I became a licensed real estate agent, the people I was working with were ready to buy a home, so I started off in the business with a bang! When I became a real estate agent, I needed to work with lenders, and I didn't forget Debbie Currie who had mentored me in the lending business. She and I became a powerhouse team, where I would sell the houses and she would set up the loans for them. We made *so* much money together! Besides that we were the best of friends. We'd have lunch, go to dinner together, go shopping—we did all sorts of things together. Even to this day we still have each other's back! Just in case anyone's interested, Debbie still works as a lender at Cherry Creek Mortgage in Wisconsin.

I was so busy in real estate (and so successful) that people were noticing me in the business. One day I went into an office for Shorewest Realty, the biggest real estate company in Wisconsin. They had franchises all over the state. I was there to set up a showing for one of their listings, and out comes Luddie Holmes. She was the chief manager of that office. She had been working there for years, she was an extremely educated, good-spirited Christian black woman and I absolutely fell in love with her. She said, "I've been hearing about you. Come into my office and let's talk." (Do you see God?) She totally sold me on her company, so I quit my current job and immediately started working for this company. She taught me all the ins and outs about the real estate business, and within a year I quickly became one their top agents. Favor was all over me! I remember meeting and working with another one the top agents named Dionne Barnes. She'd say, "Let's have a contest. How many houses are you going to sell this month?" and I'd say "fifteen," and she'd say, "Fifteen it is," and by the end of the month, we both sold fifteen or over. Favor isn't fair.

Lamont's Death

Things were really going well for me. I had since moved into my own five-level condo, and my brother-in-law, my sister, and I would fly all over the world. You see, my brother-in-law worked for United Airlines and would get "buddy passes" which allowed employees and their families to fly and just pay for taxes. We went to places such as Hawaii, Las Vegas, Puerto Rico, California—just to name a few. Every year on my birthday, February 3rd, and my sister's birthday, January 28th, her husband would take us anywhere we wanted to go. I miss that. This is the last card my sister bought me for my birthday on the last trip we took together.

On the outside it said:
My courage, my confidante, my friend, my serenity, my saving grace, my sister.

On the inside:
When I think of the memories I cherish most, full of laughter and tears and everything in between, you are at the heart of all of them—my sister, my friend for life. Happy Birthday

and she signed it:
Happy Birthday Lil. Love and God bless, Tina.

I remember the last time he took us somewhere and we had just arrived back. We called my mother to let her know we were on our way to her house and she told us to go directly to the hospital. When we got there, we found out my oldest brother Lamont, who had a stroke three years earlier, was gravely ill.

While we were at the hospital, Scotty, his son (Lamont Junior), told everyone that Lamont's current wife, who had dropped him off at my parents' house and abandoned him there, better not show up at the hospital. She didn't. Later on that night we received a call from the doctor and he told us Lamont had passed and asked if we would all like to come and see him. Everyone said no. I always felt guilty about that.

On the day of Lamont's funeral, a fierce snow storm suddenly appeared and it ended just as suddenly when the funeral was over. It was as if he was trying to tell us something.

Standing at the casket, the things I'll always remember are how tired he was days before his stroke, his words "I just wish I had some adult conversation," and how he always asked me to pray with him. I felt regret. If only there were something I could have done. I should have appreciated the time we had together. The only thing I don't regret is praying with him. At least I did that.

During the viewing of the remains, his wife showed up without welcome. The reason it was so insulting to Lamont and the rest of my family is because she abandoned him at my mom's house and now I saw her at the funeral, falling all over the casket, crying and carrying on so dramatically. I thought, *Why is she acting like she's grieving when we all knew she is happy he's gone?* We all knew it was all an act, so when it was our turn to view the remains, my mother and I ignored her antics and simply stepped over her as she lay sobbing on the floor at the foot of the casket. When we were done viewing the casket, we both went back to our seats as if she wasn't even there; we didn't even offer to help her up.

After Lamont's funeral, even though the snow stopped, it was so cold, and at the graveyard they didn't have a hole dug yet to lower the casket into, so they just had it set up over solid ground. It was a very nice military funeral. After the gravesite service was over and as everyone walked away, I looked back and saw his casket sitting there all by itself, so all alone above ground in the cold. Everyone had gone now and all was quiet except for the sound of the freezing wind. I knew he was dead, but I couldn't help but think he must be so cold. Couldn't someone at least put on a blanket? It was so unfair that after all that had happened to him and after everything was taken from him that now he didn't even have an open grave to be lowered into with a blanket of dirt to take him out of the cold.

I believe something can be learned from what happened to my brother Lamont: no matter how good you are or how happy a family you have, the enemy wants to destroy and kill. A demon in the form of another woman (or man) can come in and destroy all that is good if you let it.

In our younger days, Lamont was a happy-go-lucky big brother. He was the nicest brother and nicest guy you could ever meet. He was honest, he would go to work every day during the week, and on weekends his friends, family, and I would come over, have a few beers, and play bid whist. He had a loving wife and son. I remember my family and his were like best friends and we'd take turns staying over at each other's houses. Life was good and happy. We didn't know it at the time, but a demon was coming for him.

It all started when Teen his wife said she would get these strange phone calls while Lamont was out. The phone would ring, Teen would pick it up, and it would hang up on the other end. At the time, nobody believed her about how many of these calls she'd get.

Later on, we noticed that Lamont's drinking habits began to change. He normally only drank on weekends, but now his weekend drinking extended to more and more other days of the week.

We didn't know it at first, but another woman had crept into his life. She got him to begin living a party lifestyle and eventually got him to leave his wife and son, Lamont Jr. She then got him to move out and buy her a house for them to live in. She had many friends and relatives who constantly came over and partied and stayed for days and weeks.

Eventually, the lifestyle he had moved into took its toll on him. It became too much for him to take. He was no longer the happy-go-lucky, nice, hardworking, energetic guy. He was now tired—so tired all the time—and that's when he met me at my mother's house that day.

My Confidant, My Friend, My Sister Tina is Dead

After Lamont's funeral, my sister Tina and I decided to buy some buildings in Milwaukee and rent them out. My good friend, Billy, who was a fellow realtor, and her husband, an investor, owned about fifteen buildings; they were going to move out of state and Tina and I were going to buy some of them. Tina's credit was better than mine, so we decided she would put them in her name. I remember, before Billy moved out of town, we went on a trip to Las Vegas together. We laughed together and had such a good time there. Billy used to like to dare people to do things, and I remember on our Vegas trip, she saw this limo with a bunch of white people inside, and she dared me to jump into their limo for 100 dollars—and of course I did it! I remember the initial shock on the limo passengers' faces! Then everyone laughed. They even asked me if I wanted to go with them!

That was the last trip we ever made together, because only six months after my brother died, my buddy, my best friend, my travelling companion, my sister, died of a brain aneurism. I thought to myself, *Two siblings within six months? Why is this happening to my family? It's like we're being punished.* I remember that day so clearly: I went out with my girlfriends, partying, and everyone in my family was looking for me.

I had just moved into my new five-level condo in Milwaukee, and my sister and her husband came from Denver where they lived and stopped at my condo with plans for us to drive to Chicago to go to her sister-in-law's birthday party. I didn't feel well, so I declined to go and they went on their own. We made it a tradition to talk on the phone every Sunday. She talked about how proud of me she was, about me getting this condo, how beautiful it was.

Two weeks later, that Sunday, we didn't talk. She called Monday and we talked for hours, laughing and acting silly. The last thing she said to me was, "You ain't talking about nothin'. I'm gonna go." And she hung up.

The next night I went out and partied with my friends, which I rarely did a lot of, but my friend Billy was with me. At 11:00 p.m., I suddenly fell to the floor and started crying. My friends said, "What are you doing? Why did you start crying?"

I said, "I don't know. I just do things like that sometimes"—this I had actually never done before—and then I got back up and continued partying. I went home and was so intoxicated I didn't notice the phone ringing all night. Around 6:00 a.m. that morning, I finally answered the phone. It was Tina's friend Shirley and she said, "Where have you been? Everyone's trying to reach you!"

I said, "I was kickin' it with my friends."

She said, "Last night around 11:00 p.m., Tina went to the bathroom with a headache, and on her way back to the bedroom, her husband said she passed out. [Do you notice this is the exact time I fell to the floor and burst into tears at that bar? My sister and I were *that* connected.] They called the ambulance and took her to the hospital. From there they airlifted her by helicopter to another hospital. It doesn't look good." I immediately hung up and called my parents, and they said I needed to come home. I then got dressed and drove to Chicago to my parents' house. From there I got on the first available plane to Denver. When I got off the plane, I got a phone call from my father. He said, "Where are you?"

I said, "I'm at the airport. I just got off the plane."

He said, "Take your time. She didn't make it." If you want to know how I felt—*I wanted to die.*

A positive from all of this, now that I think of it, is my sister may have passed away, but at least she lived long enough to see me get on my feet because of her and stay there.

Tina had two funerals: one in Denver where she lived with her husband and one in Chicago. I had to plan both and attend both of them as well. Can you imagine? I thought, *Come on! Two funerals for my best friend and sister? And only six months after burying my brother?* I couldn't believe it. I was dumbfounded. I felt like God was personally punishing me for all those things I did in the past. The Bible says God won't put on you more than you can bear but, forgive me, Father, how much more could I take? Only God gave me the strength to get through it all.

At the second funeral in Chicago where we had her remains sent to be buried there, this little girl walked up to me, pointed her finger at me and said, "You're gonna preach the Gospel!"

I said, "What did you say?"

And she said it again. "You're gonna preach the Gospel!"

I said, "I ain't gonna preach no Gospel!" I thought to myself, *At this time, why is this kid messing with me?*

After burying Tina, her only son, Thomas Blackwell, who had lost his father years earlier, moved from Denver into my condo with me in Brown Deer Wisconsin.

Bible Studies

This is how I know fasting and praying works: I was fasting and praying all week and one Wednesday, my bible study night, I asked God, "Lord. If you hear my prayer, when I get to Bible study class have Rev. Boyd talk about something completely different than his usual sequence."

During Bible study, Rev. Boyd said, "The Lord spoke to me and said someone in this class wants me to talk about something different tonight, and so that is what I'm going to do. Is there anyone in the class who wants me to talk about something different?" I was in shock! He was going to talk about something else like I had asked God! I was too scared to admit I was the one who had prayed for a different subject. After class, I told Rev. Boyd I was the one who wanted the different subject and he said, "I'm glad you told me because now I know God told me to do that. I don't want the people to think I'm going nuts."

Sunday School Teacher and Choir

Tom and I both had joined an acting school because we were both interested in acting. One reason I knew I'd be a good actor was because of the kind of pranks I'd play. For example, I remember before my friend Julie died, sometimes I would invite her and her sister to eat at a buffet restaurant, and when we were in line for the cashier, I'd say, "I'll pay! I'll pay!" When we got to the cashier, they would point to me and say "She's paying" but then I would go into my "acting mode." I would act hysterical and tell the cashier, "Please call the police! I don't know these people!" The cashier would always believe me because I was so convincing an actress. I'd start to laugh when the cashier would prepare to call the police, and my friends would get so mad at me! After a while, they wouldn't go to restaurants with me anymore. They would always tell me, "You missed your calling."

While attending my acting school, they announced a contest where they would select some of their students to send to an acting competition with over 3000 contestants in California. I received an honorary mention award for my monologue, playing the grandma in *A Raisin in the Sun.* I was on cloud nine doing that because I always wanted to be an actress. This was one of the best weeks of my life. Soon after that, I joined a theater group.

Enter the Bishop

I remember I was attending a function around someone running for a political office in Milwaukee, and I met a lady named Charlene. It just so happens that years later, Charlene's son, Excel, would end up marrying my daughter (and they still are married today). Not only did Charlene work for the school board, but she was also guest co-host on a Gospel TV show. While talking with her, I mentioned my acting ability and experience and she said, "Oh! You'd be great on the Gospel show! I need to introduce you to Charles McMillion, the producer and host of the show!" One weekend, I went to the studio with her, and that's when I met Charles McMillion.

We hit it off, and so for the next five years, host Charles McMillion and I, his guest host, closed our show every Sunday night with, "It's just the two of us." Charles and I got along so well that he even allowed me to have my own five-minute segment called *Take Five with Lydia*, where I would interview guests. There was one particular guest who was closest to my heart. She was a young seven-year-old girl with cancer. I remember before we went on air, she was uncontrollably active, running around the studio, looking at everything, climbing around the cameras, climbing around the furniture. We had the hardest time catching her in time to sit her down and start the show. The sad part about it was that she died not too long after the interview.

I loved doing that TV show! I remember always being late—running through the news studio to get to my set in time. I remember hearing the countdown from the camera person 5, 4, 3, and Charles glaring at me like, "You better come on!" I'd throw my purse onto the chair and I'd always stand next to him and grab my microphone just in time, where Charles would say, "Hello. Welcome to Gospel (whatever year it was). I'm your host, Charles McMillion," and I'd say, "And I'm Lydia Davis." And there, he and I would spend the next hour on and off camera for the duration of the show.

I can honestly say I loved it! Every week everyone would see me running late through the newsroom to the Gospel show, and everyone would say, "There's Lydia! Late again! Hi Lydia!" We'd all laugh and I'd say, "Hi!"

The anchor, the weather man—everyone knew me. One time they asked if I wanted to be on the news and I shyly said, "No. That's okay." This was my favorite time of my life. I enjoyed being recognized at the store and on the street. I enjoyed it enough that I could deal with my grief over the deaths of my siblings. My TV career even led me to do a radio show.

Charles McMillion trusted me so much that when he couldn't be at the studio for some reason, he would let me host the show alone.

Charles and I came on the air every Sunday, and that is how I met my third husband, the bishop.

Being free from drug dependency was like walking into the brightest day, breathing in crisp new air and being washed in warm rain from heaven. I was on a new journey, and I was determined to live out my vow to the Lord—That I'd serve him until I die.

It turns out that the bishop had been watching the show (the Gospel TV show) faithfully every week, so he was quite familiar with it. One day he actually called me because he wanted to do a commercial and go live on the air. He left a message for me to call him back but never said what he wanted. For some reason my immediate response was, "I'm not calling that man back. I'm not doing that." But he called me again, this time asking if I'd meet with him because he really wanted to get some airtime. Finally, I reluctantly agreed. God's blessings were on me for sure. When I became prosperous, interested men were coming out of the woodwork wanting to date me—Doctors, lawyers, deacons, weather men. But I had no man or financial problems. I was happy with it being just me and God.

I agreed to meet the bishop at a restaurant one day to see if our station could satisfy his need for airtime and I was on my way to meet him to discuss this with him. Before I arrived I started thinking about all these men who were suddenly talking up to me and trying to date me. And they were successful and important men too!—Doctors, lawyers and deacons. They knew me from the TV show, church, or real estate. I even met a very handsome black doctor who I once invited to my house. (Occasionally I still hear from him and have to tell him I'm married.) I asked God, *Where are all these men coming from that's been trying to date me? Lord, if you want me to have one of these men give me a sign, let's use a password. Make it 45. That's it! Forty-five will be our password!*

There I was, waiting for him at the restaurant, as he was late. He finally arrived with his armor bearer, which is an assistant that must have a deep-down sense of respect for their leader, and acceptance for and tolerance of their leader's personality and his way of doing things. They must instinctively understand their leader's thoughts. They must walk in agreement with and submit to their leader and must possess endless strength so as to thrust, press, and force their way onward without giving way under harsh treatment. In the church world most preachers, pastors, and bishops have an armor bearer. No matter where that church leader goes, the armor bearer is there. So there we sat, the three of us. There were silly niceties right off. I immediately said, "Excuse me for how I'm looking today. I'm just getting over a cold."

He responded, "That's okay, I look like that sometimes, too, and I'm forty-five!"

I thought, *Oh, my god! That's the password!* And he was driving a white Cadillac and I was too! Then I said, *Okay, Lord, if this is really him, make him say it again when it makes no sense.* Two or three weeks later, he said it again, right out of the blue. That's when I was convinced. I said, *Lord, this is him! He's the one! I know we met on business, but he could also be the one!*

Ultimately, I guess you can say we got on a track that announced our mutual interest. I even began visiting his church and he had begun to ask me to go out with him a lot. The only problem with that was we had the company of his mother every time, not the armor bearer. The only time we had gone out alone, we had snuck out and went to the movies. When his mother found out, she was so furious she didn't speak to us for a week. There was nothing we did where his mother was not with us. He used to tell me that his mom covered us; no one could say we were off doing things we shouldn't. Her presence made us seem sexless! Don't get me wrong: I loved his mother with all my heart and I welcomed her being with us.

Cynthia Dies

I remember one day the bishop's mother and I were going to the flea market to buy some vegetables, and I got a call from Chicago, notifying me they were taking my baby sister to the hospital. I loved Cynthia. She was eleven years younger than me. She was sweet, she was humble, mild mannered, and she was my mom's right hand. She was the baby. Out of all of us, she lived the most normal life. I remember growing up when my mom would go to work and my older sister Tina and I would have to take turns scrubbing her diapers on the scrub board. Everyone loved Cynthia.

I remember a week before that phone call, my mother, my sister-in-law Lena, and I went out shopping, and when we came home we asked Cynthia, "Why didn't you wash the dishes? We want to cook and we need the dishes washed."

She said, "I didn't feel well." And she washed the dishes anyway. The next day I went back to Milwaukee. The day after that my mother took her to the doctor, and they said she had a urinary tract infection, gave her some medication, and sent her home. Three days later, she still didn't feel well, so my parents took her back to the hospital. While my parents were sitting in the waiting room, the doctor came out and told them, "I think you better come in. She's not looking good. I don't think she's gonna make it." My parents thought, *She's not gonna make it? With just a urinary tract infection?* What a shock! How could this be!

While packing at home, I received a phone call from my brother, Jerome, and he told me Cynthia had died of a heart attack at the age of 39. Cynthia left four kids: Dre, Loris, Chirra, and three-year-old Kyran. We were devastated.

Jerome later told me when Cynthia was on her way to the hospital the last time, she told him to take care of her kids.

It was as if she knew she wasn't coming back. This was one time I was glad to have the bishop's mother around because she really helped me through my grief. I really did love her and I still love her.

New House

One day the bishop mentioned that we'd need a bigger house if he and his foster son were to move in with me. I knew we were going to get married (I just didn't know when), so I said, "Well, we can look for one." So we began looking.

Looking back, I don't know what I was thinking. I lived in a five-level condo with three bedrooms and two full bathrooms with my nephew and my dog. I had a swimming pool, tennis courts, workout and exercise room and dog run. I was happy.

The bishop diligently went house hunting with me because I let him know that I was willing to give up my condominium and buy our marriage home. Not only did he have no problem house hunting with me, but at times he'd look for me when I had to work. So, that is how my plan to buy a house turned into my opting to buy our marriage home. My nephew Tom, my sister's son, begged me not to move in with nor marry the bishop. I told Tom I wasn't going to abandon him and said he could come with me. He said, "I'm not going to move in with you. I don't like him. Something is not right with him." No matter how I begged him, he wouldn't come with us. We decided he would stay in my five-story condo until I sold it, and he would get a condo of his own. I thought at the time that my nephew was just jealous of my new potential husband, or perhaps it was because he had just recently lost his mother and he didn't want to lose me too. I felt bad that I was leaving my nephew all alone, so I decided to give him my dog, Tickie. Tickie was the sweetest dog you could ever want to meet. He was a miniature greyhound, and when I had got him, he had been beaten and abused in the past. As a result of the abuse, he had seizures and lost all his teeth as well. In the future, be looking out for more on Tickie the seizure dog in his own series of novels.

The next thing I did was to move into my gorgeous new house. It had five bedrooms and four bathrooms. It had a huge family room, a rec-room, and an office. It was over 3000 square feet! Did I say it was gorgeous?

Soon after I moved in, the bishop sat me down on the couch and said it was time for us to get married. When it came time to tell the church about our pending marriage that we should do it in a hurry because, he said, there were a lot of jealous people in the church and he didn't want anyone interfering with our relationship. We were married on January 15th.

Christmas Surprise

During that same year, around the Christmas season, my entire family converged on Milwaukee. Unbeknownst to me, the bishop had contacted them to come for a Christmas surprise for me! On the following Sunday after my family's arrival, they were all in service, as well as myself, the big surprise pending. The bishop preached the best sermon I ever heard him preach. After the sermon, he called his armor bearer up and whispered something to him, but everyone heard him say, "Bring her to me." And the armor bearer started slowly walking down the center aisle, looking carefully at every woman, and when he got to me he kept walking and waited until he got two rows ahead of me. Then he stopped and turned around and came back to the aisle where I was sitting and very politely asked, "Would you please come up to the front with me?" He then took my hand and he took me to where the bishop was standing, following his sermon. He took my hand and put it in the bishop's hand, and that's when the bishop got down on his knee and asked me to marry him in front of the whole congregation.

My family had known that's what he had planned, thus their trip there. I was outdone, as was every other woman in the pews looking on. The next Sunday the majority of those women were gone, the church practically emptied out of obviously hopeful women. I blushed like a little girl receiving her first kiss as he slipped the engagement ring on my finger and hugged me respectfully as I accepted.

I remember him asking me to marry him at my new house I had just bought, but I never expected him to propose to me in church in front of everyone.

The Wedding Day

Two weeks later we had the most beautiful wedding at the church. It was in the heart of the winter. The colors were white and lavender. The church was packed because nobody could believe he was marrying me, so they came to see for themselves. That morning, he had his normal service, where he preached in his usual manner. At this point, the other ladies, who felt they were in waiting, still felt they had a shot at the bishop. I didn't attend the morning service because I was at home, preparing for the wedding ceremony. Just before the ceremony, the bishop was standing at the front of the sanctuary with the groomsmen, and I was in the hallway with his sister, the maid of honor and bridesmaids (my daughters) awaiting my song selection, which would have been my cue to enter the sanctuary. The singer was a woman who was a friend of the family for years. She was like family, I was told. She was supposed to sing the song to open the ceremony. The next thing I know, the singing stopped in the middle of the song, and I saw her run past me with her hands over her face, sobbing! I thought to myself, *What's going on?* Someone came into the hallway and said the wedding was to continue, and so we did. I walked down the aisle and got married. After the ceremony a friend of mine came up to me and said, "Did you see that?"

I said, "Yeah! I saw her! That girl was really sick!"

"She wasn't sick," my friend said. "She was upset because the bishop was getting married! That was a sign I didn't want to see!"

Up to this point, the bishop didn't really live at my new house, but he was there all the time—even when I wasn't there. He had keys. I remember one morning I woke up, and he was standing there in the bedroom. That scared the stink out of me! I said, "What are you doing here!?" He laughingly said, "It's my house too, now!" The next thing I knew, we would be practicing our "marital duties" even though we weren't married yet. You never could make me believe he was fooling around because, Lord forgive us, we did it all the time! He wanted for nothing! And I do mean nothing! I made sure he had everything he wanted.

After our marriage, the bishop and his adopted/foster son, who was now *our* son, officially moved in. We both loved him dearly. Once we were married, the bishop had to tell the social worker in charge of the foster son's case he was now married and had moved to another address. The social worker said she was going to have to visit our new house to verify it was an approved environment to raise a foster child. When she came over and saw the gorgeous house and lavish surroundings, and how well-to-do I appeared, and that I was in school for a college degree, her jealousy showed on her face. I knew something was wrong but didn't know what. When she was done looking carefully at everything and glaring at me, she left and called the foster son's aunt and asked if she wanted the foster son. When the aunt said yes, the social worker started proceedings to take the foster son away from us. She even came back to our house with her manager for a second visit to enlist her help in taking our foster son. I asked the manager how our lavish home and exclusive neighborhood could be an unsuitable environment to raise a foster child and told her the social worker was jealous and wanted my husband. I believe in my heart that she had slept with my husband before. The bishop and I fought hard to keep him, but because of the jealous social worker, the state felt it would be better for the foster son to live with his aunt and his other siblings.

This hurt the bishop to the point that he would cry many nights. Up until then I had never seen or heard my husband cry. I truly miss him (the foster son), and I will always love him. To this day I still long for him. He had become my boy—my son, our son

The Bishop's Wife

A typical week in the life of being Mrs. The Bishop would start on a Saturday night: I'd pick out the clothes he'd wear that Sunday. Of course I'd line all the accessories that would go with the suit too. I'd iron his shirt also. Privacy was important before Sunday ministry time, so I left him alone and could not spend any wonderful lazy days just relaxing with him. He would put in his requests and I'd fill them. Many times I'd have my grandchildren over as well, so I had to keep them quiet so as not to disturb him. On Sunday morning, I was in charge of preparing several people for church, including myself.

On Sunday morning everything was done for him: I shaved him, laid out his clothes, and every single detail in between. I monitored his bath to ensure he would get out of the tub in time to get dressed and be out the door on time. Of course I drove him to church and did not part my lips most of the time during the whole ride because he was meditating on his sermon. Now, once we got inside the church, there could be no talking still because he needed that time for total focus.

A year or so into our marriage, my husband had come home and gone to the mailbox. I happened to look out the window to see that he was retrieving the mail from the mailbox, then hid one of the pieces of mail before he came back into the house. When he came through the door, I asked, "What is that you're hiding?"

"Oh, that's nothing," he responded.

"Yes, it is. What is that? It's just mail, so what is it?"

Well, it turns out that it was a letter to him from a woman from another state. "How is a woman writing you from another state?"

"I don't know," he said like a frustrated teenager.

"Well, how did she get our address?"

"I don't know!" he lied.

I took the letter and saw that her phone number was on it. I called her and didn't have nice things to say to her either. But in return she gave me an earful! She said to me, "Lady, you don't know your husband. You don't know who you are married to!" I came to find that this woman had more knowledge about him than I did because everything she told me was the truth—but at that time I couldn't see it. Now, not only was I raped but I also had a husband that was molesting women. I need to wake up!

Evangelist Incident

Another incident involved an evangelist at the church who accused him of groping her. This was a married, faithful member of our church. As I recalled, this was the same lady evangelist who'd been calling our house like crazy. If she didn't call, she'd have her husband call. It was nonstop. My husband's excuse was that the lady was stalking him, and I believed him. One Sunday, it was my birthday, and we were tag-teaming preaching. I preached first and he ended the sermon. While I was toward the end of my sermon, I noticed out of the corner of my eye a uniformed police officer standing at the back of the sanctuary of the church, slowly moving toward the front. When my sermon was done, I went down to greet him. He said he needed to speak to the bishop, and I took him to the back office. That's when I found out she and her husband were waiting in the back of a squad car with another officer, and the reason they were all there was to arrest the bishop for sexual assault—on my birthday! He wasn't arrested and of course he denied it and I believed him. This matter escalated out of control, resulting in us having to go to court to settle the matter. I was the faithful, doting wife who stood before the judge in defense of my husband. My husband would never do such a thing, I'd said. The case ended up being a farce and the judge told us to stop airing our dirty laundry in public and dismissed the case.

Of course, later, it only made sense that this couple was trying to get to the bottom of this matter of sexual harassment from my husband toward her, because surely if a woman is stalking someone, her husband certainly wouldn't get involved too! Her husband was trying to protect his wife, of course. Why else would he also be calling the house?

Not long afterward I remember one time I was at the grocery store, and the evangelist we had to go to court for saw me there. I then noticed her as she quickly walked out the store door towards her car. She then brought her husband back into the store and came up to me and said, "I'm sorry for everything. I was not stalking your husband. He was after me. Please believe me, please! I didn't want to cause trouble. I just wanted it to come out what kind of man you were married to." And as she left with tears in her eyes, she said, "Please, please forgive me." At that moment I believed her.

Now I think we need to stop here for a second. We as women (and men too) need to stop thinking that once we marry, he or she is going to change. Face it, that's not going to happen! Because if God hasn't changed him or her, what makes us think we can?

I wanted to believe that 45 was the answer to my prayer. I contstantly ask God "Why didn't he stop him from saying the password?—twice?" So there I was: blaming God. No matter how many times women would come up to me and tell me my husband was unfaithful, I wanted to believe he was innocent, and wanted to believe God sent him. I was so humiliated.

There were many times I'd see and not see. There were matters that I'd ignore, perhaps out of blissful love or heavy exhaustion. For instance, during a particular sermon, I noticed a very nice-looking lady showing up to our service. I saw her again and again the following weeks at other services, and I never knew who she was. One day at the ending of a service, the bishop left the pulpit and went to the back office while church members were still hanging around, and the nice-looking lady stopped me and asked to join the church. I then went in the back office where the bishop and some of his family were and said, "This very nice-looking light-skinned woman who's been coming every week wants to join our church. Does anybody know who this woman is?" The room fell eerily silent, and they were looking at each other. I had to ask several times before anyone would say anything. The bishop finally said, "It's my first wife." Afterwhich he told me to open the door to the church to her.

I said angrily, "You mean to tell me you knew who she was and that she was coming to our church all this time and you didn't tell me until now?" I was shattered. I asked, "Why can't *you* do it?"

He said, "She asked *you*. *You* go open the doors to the church to her." I said I couldn't do it. I didn't feel right about it. His answer was, "Would Christ do someone like that?" He was very slick at manipulating me. I told him I would open the doors of the church to her, but he had to promise me he would never put her in any leadership position, and he promised me he wouldn't. I ended up opening the doors of the church to her because I didn't want to deny someone entry to the house of God. I understand now what was going on. He wanted me to do it because then people would think I did it on my own, without his knowledge, thus letting him off the hook. If he did it, everyone who knew them would know he was inviting his ex-wife into his church, despite being remarried, and that would start gossip. After that I no longer felt comfortable at that church. This church no longer felt like my home.

Christian Academy

Right after that, I started my own real estate company called Lydia's Realty Group. Within a year of opening my company with a total of nine agents, the market had dropped so terribly I could no longer afford rent on the office. That's when bishop and I decided it was time to open our Christian academy. That too was like a divine order from God, because my husband tried for years to open a school but couldn't get it off the ground. But it just so happens I knew someone who worked for the school board (my son-in-law's mother), and through that person I was able to get a full-blown public school building that wasn't being used that was around the corner from our church. Furthermore, our church was attached to a high school building that wasn't being used, and we got that too! So once we got it all off the ground, we had not only a K4 through 8th grade school, but also the school attached to the church which covered 9th grade to 12th grade. We offered two-shift day care, in-house suspension, full day K4 and K5, small class sizes, as well as a great sports program. We also had certified teachers and an after school program. Our school offered wood shop, home economics, foreign language, and pre-college classes. We got a group of people together and worked tirelessly, recruiting staff as well as students. My husband had a lot of faith in me. He knew if he put me in charge of things, I'd get it done. He had me doing all the hiring and firing of staff members, ordering supplies, food for the cafeteria, and working with the state for certifications. I loved it! I especially loved the children! During this time, the church was still growing. Some of the parents of the students would start attending our church.

One day, this lady came to our school trying to sell us something (I don't remember what), but after I talked to her, she said she knew a couple of people we really should meet.

She said they would be a perfect fit with us. Their names were Mr. and Mrs. Brown.

They ran another school as both owner and administrators of that school which needed repairs. Their students needed a place to go while this repair work was being done, and so they not only gave us their 80 high school students but worked with us at our schools. They had run a number of schools for many years and shared their vast wisdom and experience with us. I absolutely loved the Browns. Mrs. Brown and I became great friends. I would just light up when she entered the room, and we spent many hours laughing together. They were the most wonderful people I knew. They were the closest people to me since the bishop came into my life and I lost my sisters.

I still remember the day we were introduced to the Browns. The moment Mrs. Brown and I saw each other, we hit it off and I knew we'd be sisters in Christ.

Together, the bishop and I took them on a tour of the schools and when we got to the church, the bishop and Mr. Brown went off to discuss various things and I took Mrs. Brown and the woman who introduced us on a tour of our large cavernous old Catholic church that we rented. None of the lights were on when we walked from the front door to the rear of the church, and we heard voices laughing and talking, like the church was filled with people. But the church was empty; nobody was there except us. We looked at each other and said, "Do you hear that? Do you hear that?" We all were in shock.

I did many things together with the Browns. In addition to schools, the Browns had owned clothing stores. One time they invited the bishop and I to Las Vegas to see a clothing design show. We got to see all the latest designs and how much stores paid for their merchandise. Not only did they show us the aspects of running schools, they showed us the ins and outs of the clothing business. I enjoyed this time so much that I felt I could be happy with the bishop as long as I had the Browns with me. In fact, Mrs. Brown allowed me to use her wholesale ID number to get all of my clothes at wholesale prices. I never had to pay full price again! At least for now. I loved Mrs.

Brown! I was one happy sister because I love clothes! Anyone who knows me knows how I love clothes!

After the trip, the Browns and I were so excited about the profession we decided to go in together to open a clothing store. We even found a location for the store and planned what we would put on the mannequins in the store window. At this time, I felt I could do anything!

The store looked like it was really going to happen. But the bishop wasn't feeling it (and them) the way I did, and I don't know why. Somehow the store never materialized, and eventually they left the church. When they left the church, they left the school and any dream of a clothing business. I was devastated. I felt terribly alone and empty to the pit of my stomach. I no longer had my sister in Christ who had my back. Nobody left to counter the onslaught against me. I felt my days of joy despite my strife with the bishop were over.

We started arguing and not getting along with each other. I had this big expensive house with a tremendous mortgage payment on it. There was no time to pet my husband and his image as the bishop. I felt he needed to contribute to the household too. So one day I asked him, in the presence of his ever-present mother, "Why don't you get a job?"

His mother interjected, "He didn't have a job when he met you, he don't need no job now." What an eye-opener that was for me. I quickly realized that this arrangement was about money. If I had not been well paid and owned all that real estate, would he have dared marry me? I wondered now.

Life on the front pew of my husband's church was very hard. I was so unhappy. At first it was nice and glamorous; everyone waited on me, served me well. However, what I found out was these young ladies were merely ladies-in-waiting—for real. They were waiting for me to trip, waiting for me to mess up. That is what they were waiting on, not me. Their guise was to wait on me, the first lady, bring me water, carry my things, etc. However, they were waiting for their turn with the bishop. Everyone thought that my position was desirous and wonderful. Don't get me wrong, there were women in the church that would have done anything for me.

They had my back, doing gossip damage control, defending me, etc. I loved them and still talk to them to this day, such as Sis. Pearlie, Sis. Karen, Sis. Marion, Sis. Therese. But one person that *didn't* have my back was my trusted armor bearer. But what she didn't know was anything she said about me to anyone came back to me. This person was so against me and so "*for* the bishop," I've decided she is not worthy of any more of my attention. She was the one I had to look out for the most. And to think I sold her a house and brought her into the church.

Yes, I looked the traditional part with my flashy hats and expensive suits in order to look the match for his position and all. But I was purchasing all these things with my own money. It's not like I was being dressed by wardrobers assigned to bishops' wives. I even bought his fancy expensive suits.

Listen, looking nice on the outside and sitting pretty on the front row didn't stop the deep-seated irritations and pains that being in that position brought. I was a person who had recovered from real low living, as my crack addiction would have it, to being chosen to be a bishop's wife, perched on the front pew of his church. I deemed it an honor and a place in his life that I could not take lightly, so I never figured it would be such a mess!

We had been married a short time when I started getting messages that my husband was doing this and that with sister so-and-so and sister whomever, and he constantly denied it. I was not always quiet on my way to church. Sometimes I would fuss so much I would become tired of hearing myself. He eventually didn't even want to ride to church in the same car as me.

The Ordination

I remember when my husband was going to be ordained an apostle. For weeks we planned for his ordination. The excitement within the church, myself, and his family was overwhelming. This was the biggest event we'd ever had at our church. The planning involved was tremendous. Catering for food had to be ordered, decorations had to be purchased and put up, invitations to the church and school members, students and parents as well as teachers and other faculty had to be printed and sent. I spent a lot of money selecting and purchasing the most beautiful matching clothing for both my husband and I.

Early that morning on the day of the ordination, my husband kept looking at me with a sad spirit about him. When I couldn't stand his sad look anymore I said, "What's with you? You should be excited. This should be the happiest day of your life!"

He hesitantly said, "Unh, some people are saying bad things about me to the apostle (who was going to ordain him)."

I said, "What are you talking about? Bad things like what?"

He said, "They're saying that I been messing around with some of the women in the church and the school. I think it was people who are jealous of me being ordained. The apostle is thinking about not ordaining me."

I couldn't believe it. "How can the apostle believe that stuff? He knows you! Him and his wife have been friends with us for years! We've been to each others' churches! We would go places together! I'm going to call the apostle about this!"

He laid in the bed and said, "No, don't call him."

But I immediately went to the other room and called the apostle. "How can you believe that stuff? How can you even think he would do that?"

The apostle said, "I have heard this from several pretty reliable sources, and I've been praying on it for weeks."

I said, "Why would you wait until now, the very day of ordination to do this?"

He said, "Lydia, I've been in deep prayer about this, and for the last couple weeks I've been meeting with your husband and with the reliable sources about this, and I just don't know if I can ordain him."

I said, "For weeks? This has been going on for the last couple of weeks and I never heard anything about this? I believe my husband. I know he wouldn't do those things. Don't you believe me? Don't you trust me."

He said, "I do trust you, but I don't think I can ordain him."

I pleaded with him. "Please! You've got to ordain him! Please! We spent so much time and money setting up this ordination event. It's not you that's ordaining him—this is from God."

The apostle said, "I will continue to pray on this and I will call you back before the service."

I know you're thinking, *How can this woman be this naïve, considering all she's been through with this man? Lydia, what will it take for you to wake up and smell the coffee as my mother always said?* But I truly believed he deserved this, and not only was I trying to save my marriage I believed that God had ordained (because the bishop knew the password. Remember? 45?), but I had also invited my family and many of my friends to this ordination. It wouldn't just be the bishop that was embarrassed; I would have been completely humiliated as well. The ceremony was scheduled for 6:00 p.m., and we arrived at the church at 5:00 p.m.

I reassured my husband. "I'm sure he'll come to ordain you. He wouldn't wait this long to tell us if anything was wrong. He would have told us by now."

At 5:30 p.m., the apostle called and said, "I have carefully prayed on this for weeks now, and I'm sorry, I just can't do it. I just can't do it."

I was so devastated and shocked and hurt. "I can't believe he would do this to us! How could he do that!" I wept until just before the service started, and then I had to pull myself together. My husband said "We WILL have this service."

I thought to myself, *How Is he going to tell everyone he wasn't going to be ordained?* During the service, I watched him intently to see how he was going to break it to everyone, but the service continued. Eventually, he called me over to where he was standing and also called one of the guest pastors over to him and told us to lay hands on him and pray. I was waiting for him to eventually stand up and make the announcement about his ordination, but it never happened. After the service, everybody went home. For weeks, some people would greet him as apostle, and he would accept it without correcting them. And that's when I saw a different part of him. The man I married was not who I thought he was. I thought to myself maybe the apostle was right because I knew in my heart the apostle would never have refused to ordain my husband if it wasn't true. When I first met my husband, I truly believed I was safe from sin. I was married to a man of God, and therefore I thought I was guaranteed to go to heaven. Remember, not all men of God are deceitful and unfaithful. My mistake was, I believed my salvation would come from a man and not God. I now see the error. Do not use the errors of men to see Christianity itself as being faulty. God and Jesus and their teachings through the Bible are perfect. It is the distortions and abuses of imperfect man that are faulty. And not all men of God distort religion for their own gain or are faulty. There are some but not many. That's why the Bible says in II Timothy, 2:15 of the King James version, "Study to show thyself approved unto God, a workman that needeth not to be ashamed, rightly dividing the word of truth." In other words, you need to know the Bible yourself so you'll be able to recognize what is right or wrong within the church and elsewhere. That is, even if a preacher says something, you'll be able to say, "That's not right! That's not what God wants!" or "That man is truly anointed."

Fed Up with Wifely Duties

Not only did the real estate market start declining, I became obsessed with watching my husband, looking for evidence that he was cheating. I wouldn't believe what anyone else told me about him; I had to see it for myself, and so I continuously watched every move he made, everywhere he went when we were together. I couldn't concentrate on what little business I had because of the turmoil within me about my husband's alleged unfaithfulness. As my business suffered, so did my income and my ability to pay the huge mortgage on that gorgeous 3000 square foot house. I eventually lost the house and had to buy another house in his name. We ended up getting a two-bedroom, one and a half bath house and had to gut-rehab it besides. Our furniture was too big for this house, so I had to sell or give away all of my furniture and buy smaller furniture. I was devastated. I was extremely unhappy.

During the service, everything had its place and time. At every post stood a woman—the offering, and sometimes they would lead prayer, etc.—and I would just sit there. One time one of them asked why I never did anything, and he said "Because she is supposed to sit there and look pretty. That is what she's supposed to do." Eventually, I did begin to have a hand in some things, to the aggravation of his family members. A round of complaints and disrespect became the norm for me in that church because battling with those woman also became the norm until I had had enough. During a peak of hurt and irritation, I stood up before the woman and spoke my mind. At one point I even wolfed that I was from the Westside of Chicago and didn't have to take "crap" from anyone including them! I got up, defiantly beat my fist against my chest and boasted, "Westside!"

Today, when I think about that, I bust out laughing. But back then it was not the proper or ladylike way to express myself. To this day they are still talking about that.

Women would come from other churches to sit in his services. Some would preach too. And with some he'd run off to do things together, even if it was visiting another ministry in another city close by. The problem was I was not included and unaware of these trips. When the time came for me to confront him about it, once again denial was his stance, and once again I felt bad for being suspicious and believed his explanations, meaning that again, I believed a lie. I didn't want to believe it. I had come too far.

I remember many Sundays during his sermons I would be sitting in my seat in the pulpit. I was often nervous, thinking about my feelings on what was happening in the church, being closely watched, etc. It got to where I couldn't hear the bishop anymore and instead got lost in looking at beautiful patterns of light that slowly moved across the ceiling of the church. The patterns would eventually move down the wall and slowly come down to the pulpit in the shapes of angels. I was mesmerized by its beauty.

After Sundays were done, we would argue about where we were going to eat. Why should we have fussed about such a thing? Once the two of us got home though, he would purposely pick a fight with me, then storm out of the house, disappearing until the wee hours of Monday morning. Then Tuesday through Thursday he would find a way to stay away from home.

Benji

One thing I had going for me during this time was my friendship with this red bird who would tap on the windowsill every morning at exactly the same time every day—7:00 a.m. I named him Benji. When Benji tapped on the window, I would open the window and feed him. I used to get so much comfort and joy from watching Benji feed and then tap on the window again as if to say "thank you" and fly off. This went on for months until one morning, Benji came to the window and then flew to a tree branch and wouldn't come back to the window, and I wondered why. It turned out a squirrel had been watching and chased Benji away and started eating the food I had set out on the windowsill. I yelled at the squirrel, "Get off my windowsill!" And the squirrel ran off, chattering angrily at me. I went outside and chased it up a tree, and the squirrel chattered at me even more. I thought to myself, *That squirrel is cussing me out!* It's like he was saying "Why can't I eat too? I have babies to feed too!" I then thought to myself, "Maybe God is telling me to be generous to all—not just chosen ones." The significance of the red bird to me is that it parallels a story I heard televangelist Joel Osteen tell about the red bird that would visit his mother when his father died, as if the bird were a representative from heaven, telling her that her late husband was okay and everything was going to be all right. I still see red birds to this day.

As a couple, the bishop and I would not do much together outside of watching a TV show or a movie. He lived on the phone; that phone was pressed to his ear the majority of the time. Our intimacy was dry and had gotten to the point of being nonexistent. Of course, after a short while, I wanted to know why I was married and having no intimacy with my husband, so I asked. His answer was, "You argue too much, I can't get myself into it." The truth soon prevailed, and I found out that he had several woman who he was being intimate with instead of me.

The Voice of God

I'll never forget one morning about six o'clock, I was awakened and heard a voice say, *Go check your husband's phone.*

I thought to myself, I don't do things like that. I would never check my husband's phone!

I felt like I heard the Lord say, *Get up and check his cell phone.* This was a time when he had actually started leaving his phone in another room. People may ask why God would ask me to look at his phone. The reason is that I had told God that I wasn't going to believe any of the gossip I was hearing from all these other women in and out of the church unless I saw the proof with my own eyes. Well, I got up, went to the room where the phone was, got his phone, took it into the bathroom, checked his text messages, and was shocked speechless. There were love notes like, "I miss you, let's meet at blah blah restaurant." Oh my God! My husband is cheating on me! I gasped. (What a revelation. Hello? Anybody home?) I ran back to the bed and lay down.

I heard again, *Get up and go check his phone.*

"Lord, I just looked at it."

Again, I heard, *Go check his phone.*

I got up again and checked it, and that's when I saw nude photos of him apparently that he texted to other ladies, or perhaps his lady of choice. And then if that wasn't enough, I saw it – something that totally blew my mind. I couldn't fathom what I was seeing. I had to send it to my best friend to see if they saw what I did so I wouldn't think I was hallucinating. My friend called me back and expressed total shock. That's when I knew I saw what I thought I saw. I asked my friend never to tell anyone and to this day it has never been revealed. I promised myself that I wouldn't reveal what I saw—I felt too ashamed. I cried for days. I was sick with grief. I thought to myself, *I have to get this information onto something I can save and present if needed to defend my honor as a wife and as a righteous person.* While I was in the bathroom, looking at his phone, somehow (it must have been God helping me) I figured out how to transfer the information from his phone to mine. That day, I got up and took my phone to Sprint and asked them if they could copy the information from my phone onto a disk or something. At first he told me he couldn't help me. When he told me he couldn't help me, I started crying hysterically and told him what was going on. He immediately downloaded my husband's information onto a memory chip and I immediately left Sprint, put the chip in the stamped, addressed envelope I brought with me, and mailed it to my trusted confidante.

The very next day I was driving to school and stopping at every red light, looking through my phone at all the things I had downloaded from his phone onto mine. Now, I know you should never drive and text, but I had that phone; I had to look again to see if it was real. Only this time I saw a prompt that said *Play*. I pushed play and the picture started moving! I was outdone, speechless and sick all at once.

At this time I was going back to school for my bachelor degree.

Now there was a prompt that said, *Open*. I was so nervous. Regardless, of course I opened it. I had to know who this woman was. Actually, I didn't want to know. Everything was unfolding so fast my head was spinning while my heart was breaking. I'd married a womanizer. I would have to say that emotional upheaval was a defining time for us as a couple; his actions toward me as his wife really began to bend. Our marriage started to decline.

When I got to school, I didn't even go to class, I just sat in both of my professors' offices and cried bitterly for 45 minutes and told them the whole story. They tried to console me as best they could and finally sent me home because I was too upset to attend class.

Losing Everything

I got to the point where I simply said to myself, "No, I can't do this anymore. I cannot spend another ten years locked up in this situation and end up leaving anyway." God had me look at that phone because he knew me. He knew I would have stayed miserable in that marriage for ten years and more, unless I truly saw the proof that he was cheating on me. I truly believed God had put us together because of that password (forty-five)—God had better things for me to do than to have me live in a lifeless, loveless, adulterous marriage.

One day I was watching televangelist Joyce Meyers and cooking, and I heard a voice call, "Lydia!" I thought it was bishop, and I called out to him and noticed he wasn't there. Then the voice called me again. I didn't know it at the time, but I think now it was God telling me he was still there looking out for me, preparing me for challenges to come.

After I watched my Mercedes being repossessed right from my own garage, our little house went into foreclosure. It was at this time I decided to have a garage sale and sold everything in the house. I decided it was time to move and start all over from scratch. The plan was that the bishop and I would move into a rented condo together, but God wasn't having it.

While all of this was happening I found out my father had been diagnosed with lung, throat, and colon cancer. He also had Parkinson's disease, dementia, and pneumonia. This was after he passed out at the house, was rushed to the hospital, and he never came back home.

I remember when they moved my father from the hospital to a rehabilitation hospital and put him on the floor where they had the most critical patients. I remember when they were wheeling him out of the ambulance and before they made it to the hospital entrance. I caught a glimpse of him, his eyes wide, as if he were studying everything, like it was the first time he ever saw the outside world. I saw him breathe in as deeply as he could, like he was trying to feel what it felt like to breathe outdoor air. I believe he knew he was never coming out of that hospital again and wanted to experience and remember what the outside world was like for one last time. It was as if he were trying to burn the images and sensations into his mind before he entered the hospital for the last time.

After this, my focus changed. While I was busy dealing with my father's health, things were turning against me in the church. I was taken out of my leadership role there and replaced by bishop's first wife, and I was no longer welcome at the church or school. I was also accused of taking school funds, but couldn't have done that—I was locked out. I didn't abandon the church nor did I take any money; I was put out, locked out, and shut out of my church, my school, and the bank.

Put Out

This all happened around the time we were losing our second house. That's when things started really getting bad between us. He would go out and I wouldn't see him until the next day. I remember getting ready to move from our second house into an apartment. He was having a revival for a week. He said he didn't want me to come to the revival because I needed to be at home, unpacking from the move to the apartment. The Sunday before the revival was the last time I ever entered into that church. Monday, he came home between 11 and 12 that night, and I said, "Where you been?" And he said after the revival, he and some other preachers went out to eat. I said, "No preachers would be out at this time of the night."

Tuesday, he came home between 12:00 and 1:00 a.m. Wednesday was Bible study night, and I decided to take a break from packing to move and come to the church. My husband said, "No, things are just fine at the church. You don't need to come. You can just keep doing what you are doing." And, like a good wife, I stayed home. That was about the time I found out his first wife, who had joined the church a year earlier, had been moved up into leadership. I realized then I had been kicked out of my church. The next couple of nights, I didn't see him at all. He said he needed a rest from me.

Two weeks before all of this happened, I suspected someone else had been sleeping in my bed, so I had a yard sale and sold almost everything in the house: the bed, furniture—anything you could sit on. I had very little left to pack, so I don't know why it took me a week to pack for our move to the apartment.

During all of this time, while my husband was at the revival, not only did I pack everything, move it to the new apartment, and unpack all by myself, I was also running back and forth to and from Chicago to attend to my father. The only time I remember the bishop doing anything for me at all was when he made some people from the church help me move.

Thursday, he had his revival and I didn't see him all night. Friday, after the revival had ended, he helped unpack for a while and then left, saying, "I need some air," and "I need a break from you." Saturday, when he came to the condo, I said, "You can take your stuff and get the heck up out of my house because you ain't staying here no more." He grabbed a week's worth of clothes and left. For the next week, he disappeared. The most I could get out of him was he said he was staying in a hotel but wouldn't tell me what hotel.

After that week, he came back and I said, "Okay, now you can get the rest of your stuff and go back where you came from." That was the end of our living together.

Locked Out

One day, I wanted to return to the school to collect my belongings, especially my brown book which contained everything I did from when the school was just a thought, to opening it, to the last piece of candy I sold at the school. I still remember when a woman I hired saw me coming toward the school to get my belongings, looked really scared, ran inside, and locked the door—locking me out. I still remember hearing the door lock from the inside. That sound broke my heart.

I remembered all that work I put into that school. I was so proud. I remember I opened a candy store, but I gave away more candy than I sold. I would give candy to kids that couldn't afford to buy it. I loved those students so much. We had a real basketball team and everything. Different schools' basketball teams would come to our school to play our team. I had started selling soda, nachos, chips, and other snacks at the games. Of course there would be kids that came to the games who couldn't afford anything to eat. I could always tell which ones couldn't afford anything because they would just stand around, looking at me. I'd pretend I didn't see them, and when I gave them food, the smiles they gave me warmed my heart. We had a good bunch of teachers that I interviewed and hired. We had an assistant principal who would give them an interview as well, but the bishop would have the last word whether to hire them or not. He always trusted my opinion, though. At the school we would serve breakfast and lunch, so it was a great responsibility. I had to order food for both of our schools. I worked with Sisco, the company that supplied food to our cafeteria. They also supplied food to several big-name restaurants. It was really a challenge to put together nourishing meals for the students when we were down to the last funds before the beginning of the next month, when the state would give us another funding draw. We all worked so hard but felt it was worth the effort because, in the end, it was all about the children.

I had one particular favorite little boy, Jawon, the son of the religious teacher who was also a bishop. He was a K4 student and those big eyes of his would completely melt my heart. I felt so close to him that when I had my grandkids over, I'd invite him too. I remember some days, Jawon would cause a little havoc in his class room just so he could be sent to the office to see me. One day he was sent to the office, and when he came, they told him he was in big trouble and the bishop was going to "get him," so he knocked on my office door (which I had three ways in or out). He came in, crying, saying, "The bishop is gonna get me! Can I please stay here?"

The bishop could be heard in a neighboring office, so I said, "Hide under my desk."

When the bishop came in, he asked me, "Where's Javon?"

I said, "I didn't see him." I remember Javon looking up at me with those adorable big eyes. When bishop left to look in other offices for him, I said, "Javon! You better get out of here! Bishop's gonna get you!" He ran out the back door to my office, and I could see him running down the hall as fast as his little feet could go and I didn't hear from him the rest of the day.

I also remember this little girl with big dimples who, every day after school would come to my office and hold her arms out for a big hug, and when I picked her up to hug her, she would kick her little feet like a fish and tell me how much she loved me. Those are the memories that made me work without pay when the money became tight. Things weren't always good at the school. There were times we had to put students out if they were a danger to the teachers or other students. There were times money was tight and I and other people working there went without pay to keep the school going. I remember coming close to the end of the school year and money was tight. We had to let some teachers go. When it was getting close to when we had to let people go, bishop would come to me and ask me to get rid of the best teachers we had. I was very suspicious of that and didn't understand his motives until later. He would conveniently not be there that day. He'd say, "You hired 'em, you fire 'em." After I fired them, bishop would hire them back so their devotion toward me would be lost and he would win their devotion instead. He was setting things up to phase me out, and when he got rid of me, everyone would be on his side and not defend me. And that's exactly what happened. It made it easier for the woman I hired to lock the school door on me. Now it was all taken away.

Our school was a real school. It had two-shift day care, in-house suspension, full-day K4 and K5 programs, a great sports program, certified teachers, and after school programs. We opened the doors every morning in prayer. I believe that's why we had very few incidents of trouble.

Other than God, I was now alone.

Shut Out

During that summer, the bishop moved in with his family and I was living in a townhouse condo.

At the end of school, he told me he realized I hadn't been paid for several pay periods, and he was going to take me to the bank and get the money.

When we got to the bank, he told me to go into the bank, fill out a withdrawal slip, and withdraw some of my missing pay while he sat in the car. I said, "No, you come in with me and you withdraw the money and give it to me." When we were at the teller, I told the teller to have him withdraw the money and give it to me.

When we left the bank, he asked me, "Why are acting like that? Why didn't you just get the money? Why did I have to go in with you?" I said, "You are paying me, so it was only right that you would be the one to withdraw the money and give it to me."

The next day I found out he had gone to the bank and took my name off the account. I was furious and asked him, "Why did you take my name off the account like I was going to steal the money?" He said it was "just something he needed to do" and it had nothing to do with me. He tried convincing me that someone was trying to take money from the account and wanted to eliminate me as a theft suspect.

Later, he came over to the condo and told me he believed that somebody was taking money out of the school bank account. I knew there were only a handful of people who had access to that account. He asked if I could go into the computer and change the account numbers. For some reason I couldn't get to it that day. A few days later he asked me again to change the account numbers. I told him, "There the numbers are—you change them!" He said "I want you to do it."

The next day, my girlfriend from the school (remember the Browns?) called me and said, "Did you hear the rumors going around the school that you stole money out of school account and that's why you haven't come back to the school?" I was shocked and said, "That's not true! In fact, that's not possible because he locked me out of the account a while ago. He's coming over today and he wants me to change some bank account numbers to help find out who's stealing from the school." She asked me, "Did you change the numbers yet?" I said no and she said, "Don't you dare touch those numbers! If money was missing and you changed those numbers from your computer at home, who's going to believe you didn't steal it?" I thought to myself, *Oh my God! We're talking federal penitentiary here! That dirty dog!*

For weeks I travelled between Milwaukee and Chicago, visiting my ailing father in the hospital. My husband never came and never prayed for him.

A New Chapter

My husband's clothes came and stayed at the condo, but he didn't. Once he had left for good, I began to grieve for him and our relationship, and eventually, through the persistence of my friend Nichole, a realtor/attorney, I looked online at a Christian dating site. I put my information in and a few days later, I got such a large response of men it scared me so much I immediately turned my computer off and didn't go back to that site. A day later, I received a phone call from an exclusive dating service that had seen me online, and I told them I wasn't interested. Then I thought about it and called them back and said I was interested. Then I called back and said I wasn't interested. After going back and forth with them, I finally decided to join. What convinced me to join was in my conversation with the dating service representative, I found out she was a recently born again Christian. That was what got me. I was told it cost 1200 dollars (the last money I had); the clientele was strictly gainfully employed middle class to well off, and they checked everyone out thoroughly, so I went on a date.

After the date with the second match, I swore I wouldn't ever do it again and I would rather stay home alone and feel sorry for myself, crying in bed every night. The dating service called me back a week later, and I said I was no longer interested. She then told me she had personally interviewed and picked out what she thought would be the perfect match and finally convinced me to continue with the service. Before my first date with this man, I decided I was going to cancel it, stay home, and continue to feel sorry for myself. My girlfriend called me and scolded me, saying, "You get yourself out of that bed and go on that date!"

I said, "No! I'm staying right here in this bed!"

My girlfriend then said, "You get out of that bed or I'm coming over and dragging you out!" I finally reluctantly decided to go on the date with the third man.

I remember that day very well. I was lying in bed and the phone rang. It was the bishop. He said, "Can I come over and take a shower?" I thought to myself, *Why do you want to take a shower here now? For the last few weeks you didn't have to shower here. You obviously had a place to shower then.* I knew he was up to something. Against my better judgment, I said, "Sure—you can come over and take your shower." He had a little clothing still over at the condo. When he came out of the shower still naked, he went into his little dance to get my attention. He stood naked in the open bathroom doorway looking into the bedroom, lotioning himself up in front of me in the fullness of his manliness. He didn't get the result he was after; I simply turned over in bed and faced the opposite direction. That was the last time I saw *that*.

This dating service worked with the restaurants and set up the reservations for the clients. During the middle of the day on a pleasant September Saturday afternoon, I entered the restaurant for my date. I was so nervous, and was fussing at my girlfriend in my mind. "I'm never doing this again! Not ever!" The waitress escorted me to my table, and there was this brown-haired, blued-eyed, distinguished-looking, well-mannered, computer engineer-guitarist named Ed. When we saw each other, we both shyly smiled, and after a glass of wine, my coat came off and we had the most wonderful time. We stayed on the date an hour longer than we were supposed to. After the date, he then politely walked me to my car and I drove off. A week later before we went on our second date, the bishop showed up while I was getting dressed up to go out. When he saw how I was dressing, he demanded, "Where are you going?" I said nervously, "I'm going on a date." He was furious and shouted "You better keep your butt in this house!" I escorted him to the door as I was leaving. Ed and I met for our second date at an installment of Milwaukee's Jazz in the Park where he had brought a picnic basket of sandwiches and wine. He told me he was raised a Catholic, was the oldest of two children and, like my father, loved jazz and in fact played bass in a jazz band. After a few dates I told him about my family situation and my father, and he struck me with how kind, gentle, and humble he was. He said if I ever needed anything he would help me. He was willing to come to Chicago to meet my family, and so while I was visiting there, I invited him.

I remember looking out the window, waiting for him from my mother's basement apartment in the west side of Chicago. There were people walking up and down the street, cars driving by with thumping loud rap music, and people selling drugs on our corner. My mother suddenly saw this man walking nervously and speedily down the street toward the apartment. She said, "That must be him! He's just flying down the sidewalk!"

I quickly ran out the front door and yelled, "Here I am!" and invited him in. He met my mother and everything went well. All the time he was there, my mother and I tried as hard as we could not to laugh at this obviously terrified man.

From there, we went to the hospital to visit my father. When we entered his room, I introduced him to Ed, and my father gave him a suspicious look as if to say, "Who is this fool you brought with you? What does he think he's gonna do with my daughter?" My father was always a good judge of character, so I was terrified, thinking to myself, *Oh no! Daddy sees something wrong with him that maybe I can't see!* All the time Ed was there, my father stared at him with the same look. That really bothered me.

I thought for sure Ed would run back to Milwaukee and never come back. Instead, he got himself a hotel room and took me out to dinner at a jazz club and treated me to the best filet mignon while listening to live jazz.

The next day, we visited my father again. As we entered the room, my father gave Ed that same suspicious look, but then I told him, "Daddy, Ed took me out last night to a jazz club and we ate the best filet mignon I ever had, and we listened to jazz to settle my nerves." His expression completely changed from a man of suspicion to a man of peace and acceptance. He even smiled at Ed and waved hello to him. He finally gave his approval! Something I never got from him with other men: Daddy's approval. I felt so much better.

The reason for my father's pleased expression when he heard about the jazz was that he was always a huge jazz fan. He was always listening to jazz and blues. I remember when my brothers and sisters and I were young, he *made* us listen to jazz. He would carefully listen to each note and say "Listen to that, girl! Can you hear that? Oh! Here's the good part!" and laugh, explaining every detail of each song.

At other visits I made without Ed, my father would even ask, "Where is that boy?" And I'd say, "He's in Milwaukee, working."

A few weeks later, my father's illness progressed to where he had stopped speaking. While visiting his room with my mother, his eyes would follow me wherever I went in the room like he was studying me—like he was seeing me for the last time. My mother asked me why he was looking at me like that. I said, "I don't know. I guess he's just looking at me."

I told him, "I have good news! I'm going to Milwaukee to pack my things and am going to move back to Chicago to take care of you and mom! Just hang on and I'll be back in a couple of days." Before I left the room, I said, "I love you," and he motioned his lips silently in the shape of "I love you." As I left, I turned to look back at him (he didn't know I was looking) and he had turned his gaze back toward the TV, staring into space. It was as if he knew it would be the last time he'd see me.

A few days later, I was told my father had gone into a coma so I was on my way back home to Chicago. I was worried about my father, I was worried about my marriage, I was worried about packing—I didn't want to move back to Chicago. I was worried about so many things, and I heard the voice of the Lord tell me, "You go home and take care of your father and let the dead bury the dead." For a long time I didn't know what God was telling me. I thought he was telling me to bury my father. I realize now that he was telling me about the bishop—that he was dead in spirit.

I remember a year after I moved back to Chicago, the bishop called me at 3:00 a.m. and said, "I need you to forgive me." I said I already forgave him, and he said again in a loud voice, "No! I need you to forgive me!" He had fallen very ill and needed me to release him by forgiving him. I now received what he was telling me. I said, "I forgive you." That seemed to give him relief and he hung up. What the bishop didn't realize until then was that I had favor with God. From the time he cleansed me from AIDS, I was one of the top insurance agents, made half a million a year as a real estate agent, became a gospel co-host on the radio, began acting, opened up my own real estate company, opened up two schools, having favor with the state for funding, and helped grow the church. When he got rid of me, he thought he could take that favor from me for his own use. But that's not how favor works. That favor was *my* favor, not his. After he got rid of me, within three months the school was closed, and later, when he became very ill, he realized he really messed up and that God does not play, especially when a man of God, his representative on earth, commits adultery, tries to frame the very woman who helped him, puts her out of the church, locks her out of the school, and shuts her out of the bank accounts. He knew then he had to have my true forgiveness to be released from God's wrath.

My mom and relatives told me the day before I got back and they were visiting my father, he suddenly opened his eyes and had the widest, brightest, happiest smile on his face they ever saw, and then he closed his eyes again for the last time. I believe he saw Jesus welcoming him, and he knew he was going home. This was hard to me.

When my father died, Ed became a pallbearer at my father's funeral.

Life for me took on a norm that leveled me and helped me to see beyond the hype of materialism. I still had my fancy clothes and no place and no reason to wear them. My new car still ran, but how would I afford to maintain it now? I had been ambushed once again, but this time crack cocaine was not an option. I'd grown away from such crutches. The love of my parents and my mother's open door was all I needed to help me back on to my feet. And how timely it all was. My mother needed me, and thank God I was there for them this time. It's good to have someone else to help through a rough time when you too are going through your own hell.

There are a lot of women in the world that are desperate to have a man to call their own; they can't wait on the God of heaven, the One who knows all and is all, the One who will grant us our partner in due time. But as you saw in my story, not waiting and not knowing the Lord can wreak havoc and death on your life and that of your children. Choosing your own partner by way of emotions is not what is intended for God's special children. He has so much more, but some of us will never know if we choose to do things our way only. I'm not saying that using your own common sense is a bad thing. We still need to run our so-called common sense through God in prayer before we step out on it alone. Of course the word of God in Proverbs 18, verse 22 says, "He who finds a wife finds a good thing." Not a woman who finds a man. See, that was my problem, and look where it got me. When recalling such accounts too often, the children that were wounded in adult choices are left out.

Our foundation plays a pivotal part in our lives and decision-making abilities as adults. My dear father was a rolling stone indeed, and I was not blind to that even then. In fact it became normal. There is no doubt in my mind that seeing my father's antics played out before my childhood affected my thoughts on men. I saw my mother put up with it and keep her family together instead of splitting us all up just to get away from him. I guess you can say, to some degree, I followed suit. But it turned out my father was the best influence I had in my life, and I know that he loved us. If it weren't for my parents, my children would have been put in a foster home. I just want to say thank you. I wanted a man that could love me and take care of me and my two daughters, regardless. However, if having a man or being in a relationship that will put your children in jeopardy is the best you can do, then WAIT! Keep the ears of your heart peeled toward heaven and listen. You will not go wrong. My message to women is that they don't need a stripper, a drug dealer, or a bishop, or any such thing because God will supply all our needs according to his riches in glory by Christ Jesus. Having your babies suffer while trying to make your own supply is never worth it. I cried and hurt for years and years over the molestation of my daughter because of my own stupidity. When I found this out, I felt like I could have died.

    I didn't need to depend on the drug dealer for my food and shelter, furniture, and feeding my children. I realize that now. There was a time in history when girls were betrothed to men after a certain age because it was the only way they'd be provided for after leaving their parents' home. They'd have babies, keep house, cook, and give plenty of sex. But that is not the case today.

    When I went to the bishop, my mistake was in thinking that marriage to him was a sure ticket into heaven, since I'd be spending my life with the Lord through him. Can you imagine that I was so naïve that I equated being with him with being with the Lord? I was convinced that I had a man I could trust; he'd be faithful, he wouldn't dare approach my grandkids wrongfully (my daughters were grown by now), and he had an excellent vision too. But it seemed I was just as bad off with the Bishop as I was with the drug dealer. I was just as willing to see his own worldly self-centered vision to fruition (not God's) while trying to raise two daughters.

Final Words From The Author

I would like to think that an outcome like mine is not uncommon for women who choose to do things their way. If I had it to do over, of course I'd wait, I'd choose better, I'd listen with my heart, not my need. Paying too much attention to your biological clock is one of the biggest deceptions of all. It's a trick of the enemy.

This was all my fault for sure. I have learned the hard way not to look to man for anything outstanding. My eyes should have been lifted to the hills where my help truly comes from: the Lord who made heaven and earth. The only outstanding things these men offered me was addictions, disease, and abuses. It cost me and my daughters our sanity for quite a while. Not to mention my mother's broken heart to see her daughter and grandchildren living a life of debauchery (in my daughter's words).

Coming from being Mrs. Stripper to Mrs. Drug Dealer and then to being the most coveted Mrs. Bishop, you would think this would be the testimony for the ages. Women began to see me as the one who made it through insurmountable odds, the woman to be like. All I see is that women have to stop looking to man and look only to God. Yes, I had friends say to me, "Are you crazy? You're going to divorce a bishop? Don't do it. Just give it time!" But my suffering preceded me, and I had to follow my heart through the strength of the Lord, my God. It's a struggle but I'm starting all over again now. I have learned things the hard way, and it tears at me to see other women out there with innocent little children who are being molested right now because they have picked up some charming man off the streets that smiled at them and told them they were pretty. At the end of all the blushing, they make a home with him and put him over their sweet children as the new daddy, only for that baby to be violated by him. All because they could not, did not, or didn't know to wait on God. There are other women being abused, beaten, raped, and set up. Sure, it is possible to meet Mr. Right as I did in an unlikely setting, marry him, and life turns out fine.

Far too many feel like they have it made because they have a church-attending man. Ladies: Do your part to attract the right man. What is in you, you will attract, and there are all kinds in the church too. I'm not talking about all men who are in the church, I'm talking about those who are living according to their fleshly desires while warming a pew, singing in a choir, ushering, preaching, and teaching. They can easily be no different than street hustlers and dealers and can take you on a ride that will alter your belief system for life.

Today I am married to a wonderful, normal guy who adores me right where I am. We mean the world to each other and serving him is my profound pleasure. Only the Lord of Heaven could have overseen this miracle, because I was done with men. My belief in them had been destroyed. The good thing is that my experiences gave me wisdom and strength to overcome my previous addictive behavior. The next time an issue or problem happens, would I turn to drugs, drinking, or sporadic behavior? No, I didn't at all; I'd been completed healed and delivered from any of the devil's remedies. My God did this, and I'm living in his glory today, and you can too!

The wounds I felt through these relationships can cause others around me great pain. I didn't want to misinterpret the actions of others through my own hurt because I know hurt people often hurt others around them by coming to distorted and maybe untrue conclusions and in turn say things or act in ways that harm others. We must always be just gracious as God is. I'm not making excuses for these men, but I'm learning that we all are imperfect. Unforgiveness, bitterness, and hatred can cause us not to live God's purpose for our lives. We must not live with unhealed wounds. Wounded people blame others for their hurt. I just don't want to have to pay twice: once for when I was wounded and again with unforgiveness. Without forgiveness, how can the Lord heal me? God gives us grace and he is merciful. He can free us I have been unforgiving to myself for years for the hurt my daughter suffered during my addiction and my daughter's molestation—I am now trying to forgive myself.

I didn't write this book to crucify anyone—Not the stripper, drug dealer, nor bishop. I wrote it to let people know that you can't get salvation through man. Salvation is only possible through God. Because man is imperfect.

Being with the stripper showed me that although I thought my happiness could be supplied by satisfying my physical and sexual needs I would later find out that his charms blinded me to dangerous character flaws that eventually brought harm to me any those I love (in my case, my daughters).

With the drug dealer, I believed that happiness could be found by material and chemical gratification, which I found to be false. Material gratification will not provide security or give you lasting happiness. Chemical gratification leads only to addiction and death.

Being with the bishop, I found that salvation could not be found through man. Man can give you the appearance of salvation, which is not true salvation, because true salvation can only be obtained through God. Proverbs 3: 5–6 says that we should "Trust in the Lord with all thine heart; and lean not unto thine own understanding. In all thy ways acknowledge him, and He shall direct your paths."

First there must be full commitment of ourselves to the Lord—spirit, soul, and body. We must trust him not only for salvation of our souls but also for direction in our lives. We must be committed to him at all times. We then must acknowledge that we don't know what's best for ourselves and that we are not capable of directing ourselves. Also we must acknowledge that Jesus Christ is our Lord. And that is in every aspect of our lives. He must have control. That is, acknowledging him in all our ways. It is doing his desire, his will, his way. There are always conditions to every promise. God's promise is to direct our path if we meet his condition of acknowledgement.

In every corner of my life, God was there. Through every negative action or event, there was a positive reaction by God. My last words to you are, "Did you see God?"

IT IS FINISHED.

$15.99
ISBN 978-0-692-98889-3

www.ingramcontent.com/pod-product-compliance
Lightning Source LLC
Chambersburg PA
CBHW060514100426
42743CB00009B/1311